Consultation Skills Readings

ROBERT J. LEE, PH.D.
AND
ARTHUR M. FREEDMAN, PH.D.
EDITORS

P.O. Box 9155, Rosslyn Station, Arlington, Virginia 22209

For information on ordering copies of this book or obtain-
ing permission to reprint articles, write to:
  Publications Department
  NTL Institute
  P.O. Box 9155, Rosslyn Station
  Arlington, Virginia 22209

Nanci Appleman Vassil, NTL program coordinator for
professional development programs, assisted in the
preparation of this book.

ISBN 0-9610392-1-3

NTL Institute

NTL Institute for Applied Behavioral Science was founded in 1947 as the National Training Laboratories. Its founders saw that changes in human behavior, values, and motivations have a profound impact on organizations, institutions, and systems, and they believed that organizations must adapt to change if they are to function effectively.

Throughout its 37-year history, NTL has come to symbolize a professional approach to leadership development for current and emerging problems. NTL's programs respond to the need for converting scientific knowledge of human behavior into practice. Corporations, government agencies, voluntary associations—groups of all kinds—require skills in collaboration, social sensitivity, and creativity. NTL seeks to help people learn to use available knowledge in gaining the ability to work effectively with others.

In its training and consultation, NTL strives to help people refine problem-solving techniques, develop skills to enact change, become aware of cultural and gender issues, become aware of the tenuous balance of man and nature in a highly technical society, and augment resources to establish conditions in which human energy—one's own and others'—becomes released willingly and creatively to achieve individual and organizational objectives.

Dr. Robert J. Lee has been an internal and external consultant since the early 1960s. Since 1974, he has been president of Lee-Hecht and Associates, a New York-based executive counseling and management consulting firm. His particular interests are in the areas of organizational effectiveness, performance measurement, and diagnostic techniques. His PhD is in industrial/organizational psychology from Case Western Reserve University.

Arthur M. Freedman lives and works in San Diego as manager, Human and Organizational Effectiveness for Management Analysis Company (MAC). The firm provides comprehensive multidisciplinary consultation and field services to such industries as electric (primarily nuclear) utilities, telecommunications, and energy. Dr. Freedman received his BS and MBA degrees from the College of Business Administration at Boston University and his PhD from the Department of Psychology at the University of Chicago. He has been an active member of NTL Institute since 1969.

Introduction

This book of readings has been collected for the use of participants in NTL Institute's Consultation Skills programs.

The reality of the consulting profession is that there is great diversity in what practitioners do, why they do it, and how they explain it to others. There is a shared core of skills and knowledge, but also many ways to expand on that core to create a personal approach to being a consultant.

The ConSkills program is a skill/theory course but also a personal ("experiential") event in which learning follows from doing. Because of the diversity of views in this book, the reader is required to select, reject, question, resolve differences, and ultimately to "work through" these materials. What each author says needs to be chewed on, not swallowed whole or rejected as a whole. Those readers who seek only to learn how a certain other consultant thinks or does her or his work will find this book of limited use (ditto for the ConSkills program itself). Readers who want ideas and raw material for building their own body of consulting skills will find plenty of material.

The papers included here have been useful to various OD (Organizational Development)/process consultants as ways to help others understand and grow. Most of these papers have been used as handouts in recent ConSkills programs.

When organizing this book we used four guidelines to meet readers' needs. First of all, we've emphasized papers on consulting, rather than on OD, process analysis, social issues, or specific organizational problem areas. Techniques and group exercises are seldom discussed. The focus is on the consultation process itself—that complex event occurring between helper and client. There is no clear line separating consulting from these other topcis, however, so there is some necessary overlap. Second, we've included materials on the personal life of the consultant, a topic often discussed in ConSkills programs. Third, there is a general flow to the chapters intended to roughly parallel the sequence of discussions in the 7-9 days of a typical ConSkills program.

Finally, we've tried to include materials not easily available in books or other published sources. We've favored items found in NTL members' 3-ring binders but seldom elsewhere. (In fact, many papers do not have authors listed because we don't know who wrote them.)

The five articles in Section I are orientation pieces. As a group they define the scope of what we're talking about when we refer to process consulting.

Section II has six papers which list and describe "the skills" of process consultants. There is, of course, no definitive list of such skills, although there is considerable agreement among these six papers. What process consultants know, think about, and do are topics that can be discussed forever without reaching consensus, yet also need more discussion than they usually receive.

Section III looks at roles. Consultants have role options within the "process" tradition, and these four short papers try to sketch some of the options.

The linear thinkers among us will especially appreciate the two papers in Section IV on stages and phases. Dividing the consulting process event is arbitrary but also helpful to many people, and necessary for some.

Contact and entry issues are presented in Section V. These key topics receive much attention in ConSkills programs, and properly so. There are many ways in which the previous discussions of skills/roles/stages actually come to life when the client is met in person for the first time.

Section VI has seven short papers on what is typically the bulk of a consultant's work: data gathering, display, and diagnosis. Library shelves are heavy with books on these topics. These papers can serve only as discussion starters.

The consulting process inevitably includes an evaluation step, or many such steps. In Section VII there are ideas on what to look for when doing an evaluation, and on how to identify causes for success/failure.

Most ConSkills participants work inside their organizations, and often work with external consultants. The first two papers in Section VIII examine the interrelationships between the two roles. The last paper somewhat in the "classic" category, examines the internal consultant role in some detail.

Section IX is on personal issues and covers marginality, anxiety, sexism, and ethics. Again, these are only thought starters, not even a good sample of what could be included under this heading. Other issues, such as racism, career planning, work/family conflicts, social activism, research and professional growth, could be discussed with equal relevance.

The last two papers are "applications" discussions which, in different ways, show how many of the other topics are pulled together to create change.

These readings are the work of many NTL members and other professionals. No overtone of "better" or "best" is implied by including papers by these people. An equally good collection could have been compiled entirely by using other people's materials. These were ones we thought would be useful, and no further endorsement is intended or implied. We hope you also find them useful.

ROBERT J. LEE
ARTHUR M. FREEDMAN
EDITORS

Table of Contents

Historical Overview of OD Consulting

Jim Shultz

After World War II, a knowledge industry arose based on the development and maintenance of organizations. Two major branches of this knowledge industry have become distinct disciplines.

Management science

1. This branch has caused the growth of masters degree in business administration programs. Management science focuses on quantitative analysis of business decisions, finance, marketing, and planning, and emphasizes economics, administration, and industrial engineering.

2. For thousands of years the world had "rulers," or leaders of large systems. By the rise of "management," I mean the rise of an applied *science*. Peter Drucker, in *The Practice of Management* (Harper & Row, 1954) sees this as a mid-twentieth-century phenomenon. The applied science of management relies heavily on quantitative analysis. (Money itself is a quantitative measure.)

3. Like applied behavioral science (ABS), management science is an applied science of organizations. Its emphasis differs from ABS, for it is more tangible and quantitative. Without the rise of management as a profession, it is difficult to imagine the rise of organization development (OD).

Applied behavioral science

During World War II, the United States government employed various academic advisors—including social psychologists and sociologists—for major interventions.

1. Stouffer, *The American Soldier*. A project to study the formation of combat teams in the Army discovered that casualties declined if training camp teams were carried over as combat teams—and therefore benefited from group development and cohesion.

2. Kurt Lewin developed force-field analysis to analyze methods attempting to get Americans to eat tripe, the best available protein under scarcity conditions.

After World War II, Lewin and his students ran a "lab" to study group dynamics. After the groups met, the scientists met to share observations. By chance, participants overheard these meetings and asked to sit in while the academic experts discussed the participants' leader-member roles. Then the participants wanted to share in the analysis. Out of this the T Group was born. The T Group created a vacuum of formal leadership and highlighted group dynamics with a cycle of participation followed by process analysis.

Lewin and his doctoral students at the Center for Group Dynamics at the Massachusetts Institute of Technology were concerned with democratic leadership. Their work from 1950 to 1970 showed a preoccupation with the autocratic-participative continuum, a continuing theme of OD.

The T Group, developed in the National Training Laboratories' (NTL Institute) Human Interaction Labs, gradually de-emphasized group dynamics and emphasized psychological processes in the 1950s and 1960s. The T-Group trainer took a more active role in creating deep psychological experiences, sometimes via nonverbal exercises. Personal growth became the focus of the T Group.

Whether it dealt with group, interpersonal, or intrapersonal identity, the core identity of NTL—and probably of all OD—was microsocial, i.e., based on small groups, not on large systems. The T-Group method included experienced-based learning and an emphasis on feelings and human relations, on individual needs, and on personal growth as exemplified in NTL's basic Human Interaction Lab.

When applied to large systems, the T-Group method investigated management style on a democratic-autocratic continuum.

1. The use of the term "democracy," a macrosocial concept best applied to nation-states, when discussing small groups sometimes backfires. The large systems that need democracy most—e.g., nations or large oligarchic corporations—are perhaps overlooked while we intervene in small, weak organizations that, lacking police power or economic strength, hardly pose a major threat to democracy and liberty.

2. Rensis Likert's System 4, Schmidt-Tannenbaum's "How To Choose a Leadership Style," and Blake and Mouton's Managerial Grid all still rely somewhat on the democratic variable.

3. The adult education movement and human relations school of management were closely tied to NTL in the 1950s. ABS spun off into conference and meeting technology throughout the U.S. and overseas.

By the early 1970s, OD theory and ABS were expanding, specializing, and proliferating:

• Personnel management grew as a field. Business schools began to offer courses in the human side of the enterprise. These gradually emerged as a distinct field called organizational behavior.

• Books by Argyris, McGregor, Bennis, Benne, Lippitt and others had a major, though perhaps short-lived, impact on management science.

• Another trend was the growth of the NTL network and the spinoff from NTL of the OD Network and IAASS, the accrediting arm of applied behavioral science.

• ABS expanded its repertiore of tools and techniques. Thousands of exercises, cases, and instruments became readily available.

— University Associates, NTL, and such authors as Fordyce and Weil (*Managing with People*) made "cookbooks" available.

— Professional training through NTL and universities trained thousands of practitioners. Group processes became part of the curriculum in social work, education, business, and professional schools.

OD practitioners (a) tended to transfer in and out of allied fields—e.g., training and personnel—and (b) tended to combine the practice of OD with line management or closely related areas.

In the 1950s and 1960s, OD built a reputation in various organizations, including long-term, large-scale programs in many large, complex organizations (private, government, and nonprofit).

— NTL's Presidents Labs brought OD to business. Organizational change often began with chief executives making a personal reevaluation and with feelings and values as well as concepts.

— With mixed results, the long-term trend was toward demonstrating an expanding repertoire of concepts and techniques.

— When human problems in organizations increased, the need for ABS approaches became more apparent. For example, affirmative action initiatives opened up new challenges for OD.

By a broad definition of the field, it included perhaps 20,000-30,000 practitioners by the late 1970s, mostly internal OD and human-resources consultants. These staff roles often overlapped with the personnel management field.

— Approximately three percent of personnel costs will probably be spent on personnel management and human resource development. So this "field" may account for $20 billion per year of gross national product. Perhaps one-tenth of this could be termed OD or ABS.

— High-technology organizations made the most extensive use of OD.

— Large, complex OD projects sometimes involved 50-100 OD-related people in various parts and levels of the same corporation, e.g., Procter & Gamble, Union Carbide, Exxon.

— More and more emphasis was placed on the interface with technical systems, e.g., job redesign, new plant design.

— The rise of sociotechnical systems (see the work of Eric Trist). Using the microsocial as a core of values, concepts, and skills, OD extended from the social system to the technical system and organizational structure and to the external systems, e.g., the market, the product mix, and social responsibility.

— OD also extended from treating parts of the organization—e.g., individuals or teams—to treating intergroups or the entire organization.

— Open-systems planning includes the total organization and its external environment as the focus of an OD process.

Is Henry Kissinger an OD specialist? Was the Marshall Plan an OD intervention? The next logical extension for applied behavioral science[1] would be to nation-states, other macrosocial systems, and international relations. The Marshall Plan was a large-system change effort based on social science, as were some of Henry Kissinger's interventions. In extending OD to the macrosocial level, do we lose the basic concepts rooted in the early NTL work on process, use of self, collaborative values, trust, experience-based learning that have defined our field—or at least our professional ideal?

Summary

The field of OD is characterized by (1) fast growth, (2) diffusion, (3) open boundaries, and (4) a wide variety of career patterns. As it proliferates it will have a weaker and weaker core mission and may eventually dissolve as a field: the subspecializations may become the only fields with which practitioners can identify as a professional reference group.

[1]The term social science is more inclusive than behavioral science. The former includes government, macroeconomics, international relations, and history; the latter, psychology, social psychology, sociology, anthropology.

Essential Differences Between Traditional Approaches to Consulting and a Collaborative Approach

John J. Sherwood

A number of years ago, a partner in a national consulting firm shared with me a growing concern he had about his own work and that of his colleagues. While Harold and the firm were by most measures very successful in terms of client satisfaction and revenue, Harold felt troubled by his increasing awareness that his clients frequently did little more than "appreciate" his recommendations. He often had contact with clients after his work with them had been completed, and at such times former clients typically expressed admiration for him and satisfaction with his contributions to their company or agency. He often heard a former client enthusiastically say, "You do fine work! We vigorously debated your first recommendation and we continue to be very impressed with the thoroughness of your report and with your understanding of our organization and our problems." When asked about what action was actually taken in light of his consultation, the response was often, "We're still considering alternatives. Some things have changed. I'll let you know what we finally decide." This left Harold feeling incomplete and believing he had not contributed as much as he could have to improve his client's effectiveness. While the client appeared to be fully satisfied, the consultant saw little consequences from his work.

This is not an unusual occurrence. Many recommendations and insights of consultants are not implemented or they are put into effect at a later time in another form. This paper presents a simple and straightforward model to ensure meaningful action from organizational consultation, and it contrasts a collaborative perspective with more traditional approaches to consulting with organizations.

Two traditional approaches to consultation

Two traditional approaches to consultation exist with which both clients and consultants are familiar and comfortable. Either (1) the client presents the consultant with a problem for solution, to which the consultant provides a recommended solution or a set of alternatives;

or (2) the client asks the consultant both to define the problem and to offer recommended solutions. This latter case is the physician's approach. The client presents a set of symptoms, and the consultant first makes a diagnosis and then prescribes a remedy. In the first approach the consultant also offers a prescription describing what the client should do to solve the problem the client set forth; for example, the consultant may design a new management-information system or an inventory-control procedure in response to a specific request from the client. The important thing to recognize in both traditional approaches to consultation is that the client is rather passive and dependent until the point at which the consultant's recommendations require implementation, and then we wonder why the client does not implement fully our solutions or recommendations.

When the chief executive contracts with a consultant to provide an inventory-control system with a certain set of characteristics, the consultant's recommendations are less likely to be fully and effectively implemented if they call for changes in customary behavior or roles that have proven useful to people in the past or if they will result in a redistribution of influence whereby some persons have more control than they had earlier. The critical question is, therefore, how to ensure meaningful implementation when recommendations require changes in valued or customary practices.

A collaborative model

In a more collaborative approach to organizational consultation, the client is the organization rather than the boss (this has important implications which are discussed below), and the client—that is, the organization—is active in all of the following phases of the consultation: (a) identification of problems; (b) conceiving solutions or actions; (c) implementation; and (d) follow-up. To say that the organization is the client means that the consultant works together with the boss to define a meaningful organizational unit—one that includes the boss—with which the consultant will work. An organizational unit could be a department, division, plant, company, agency, or the boss and his or her key staff.

A collaborative approach addresses two central issues found in any consultation (Argyris, 1970): (1) how to generate valid information and (2) how to ensure effective implementation. When increased organizational effectiveness is the standard against which consultation is evaluated, it is through decisions, based on valid information, that are actually implemented that the contributions of the consultation can be judged.

Three essential differences from traditional approaches

Collaborative consultation differs in three important ways from more traditional approaches. First, traditional approaches often assume that the client has already effectively identified the problem or that it is the consultant's responsibility to decide the nature of the client's problem. In a more collaborative approach, however, the consultant works with the client to arrive at a joint understanding of the problems facing that organization.

Second, traditional approaches frequently assume that sufficient information is already available to decide the direction the consultation will take. In a more collaborative approach, the first step is almost always to decide with the client about what information needs to be collected and from whom. These two questions are answered by learning who has the information and resources necessary to identify the problems facing the organization in meeting its objectives, who will be able to generate the most useful solutions, and who will be able to carry out those plans most fully and effectively.

Third, traditional approaches usually assume that the consultant's report or recommendations should be given directly to the person in authority (the boss) to approve, modify, and implement. In a more collaborative approach, the consultant's findings are also reported directly to the people who provided information or input during the data-gathering phase. Reporting directly to the people who provided input is a critical step in any consulting process, because these same people are probably central to any plans for implementation or action (Nadler, 1977). Furthermore, their knowledge that the organization is the client and that they will receive the consultant's findings also increases the likelihood that they will provide valid information.

When the consultant treats the organization as the client, the boss neither receives a special report nor are evaluations made of individuals for the boss. More valid information can be collected when people think they will benefit by providing accurate and complete information. When people believe that revealing concerns, problems, and dilemmas will help them do their jobs better, they eagerly share information with a consultant. When people believe that after questioning them a consultant will tell their boss how their jobs should be changed, however, they are more likely to treat the consultant with caution, just as subordinates are often careful about what information they reveal to their boss (Nadler, 1977).

A common mistake

A common mistake made both by clients and by consultants is to assume that the solution to the client's difficulties lies with the consultant. In a recent article advising potential clients how to use consultants, two practicing management consultants and a company president accept the traditional view that it is "the consultant's plan of action... which must fit your company... remember, it's the consultant's solution. [The consultant is] supposed to know what it takes to get the job done—especially in terms of judging your staff's ability to implement his program" (*INC*, 1980). While the consultant may have an acceptable answer to an organization's problems, if the outcome of the consultation is to make an enduring contribution, then a better solution generally comes from the people who must make it work (Maier, 1973).

Effective managers usually realize—or can easily be convinced—that they depend a great deal on others, both for information and for action. They also know that decisions are ultimately implemented by subordinates, not bosses. Furthermore, these executives understand how little they can do to solve the problems of their subordinates. Consultants need the same kind of humility as insightful executives in understanding that they will never know more about an organization than the collective wisdom of the people who work there. In any meeting of key personnel, those present almost always represent more than 100 years of total experience with an organization, whereas the consultant often has less than 100 hours of experience with that organization. The consultant should help members of the client organization understand that the real expertise resides in them, and it's the consultant's responsibility to help the client first generate, and then implement, effective solutions to its problems. When a particular problem calls for the application of special technical expertise that only the consultant possesses, then the consultant depends on the client to help fit the expert solution to the realities of the organization that must make the solution work on a day-to-day basis. One objective of a collaborative approach to consultation is to leave the organization more capable of identifying and managing its own problems. In this way not only is the organization more likely to realize its objectives, but it will also have less need to call upon consultative assistance from others (Steele, 1975; Miles & Schmuck, 1976).

The mistakes of consultants do not usually lie in offering inaccurate, absurd, or poorly conceived recommendations, but in not managing the consulting process adequately: that is, not providing sufficient direction and thereby letting the client flounder or taking too much responsibility at critical points and thereby stifling the client's initiative or creativity. A consultant must learn when and how to offer recommendations most productively so that his or her recommendations are (1) neither accepted naively and uncritically as coming from an expert, because thoughtless acceptance often leads to subsequent difficulties in implementing such solutions; nor are they (2) rejected without appropriate consideration because they are viewed as not fitting the unique requirements of the particular client organization. When the consultant's ideas are offered at the time when the client is struggling to decide what to do, then the consultant's suggestions are more likely to be treated for what they are probably worth—as one more alternative that one should study and consider (Argyris, 1970).

The consultation must remain a management responsibility

The consultant is often required to influence the client's expectations and behavior, that is, "to produce a good client" who takes initiative and can challenge the consultant rather than one who passively respects the expert, which is how clients frequently begin their work with a consultant. One trap for consultants is to accept exclusive responsibility for the success of the consultation. For an organization to meet its objectives more effectively, the consultation must remain a management responsibility and not be removed from the central management process of the organization. Since some degree of uncertainty always surrounds any consultation—otherwise management would not have invited a consultant to work with them—management tends to cope with the anxiety stemming from this uncertainty by conceiving of the consultation as "the consultant's project." Whenever this occurs, the consultant must "lateral the ball back to management," and then help management manage its own consultation by coaching, jointly exploring alternatives, forming task forces, or establishing steering committees. The consulting work becomes reduced in priority and impact whenever a consultant permits management to define the consulting endeavor as "the consultant's" rather than accepting it as a management responsibility.

Special treatment for the boss

While the organization may be the consultant's client, the person in authority is usually the most important person within the client organization and, as such, needs and should receive special attention. The chief executive needs to be kept abreast and should participate actively whenever appropriate, because he or she can do more than anyone else to help or hinder what is being done. For this reason, the boss is given the consultant's report *before* it is given to others. Receiving the consultant's findings in advance helps the boss work together with the consultant and subordinates in a less defensive manner.

An effective consultant builds a relationship with the chief executive because it is the boss who "sponsors" any consultation. The boss both legitimizes the consultant's

work and participates in it. In addition, the consultant insists on actively involving those persons who will be affected by outcomes of the consultation. The consultant solicits their input, then provides them a meaningful role in action planning and implementation. In a collaborative model, the consultant often works with task forces charged with studying particular problems, creating solutions, and making recommendations to top management.

Continuous concern with implementation

For a consulting effort to make a sustained contribution to increasing organizational effectiveness, the consultant must be continuously concerned with meaningful implementation. The essential task of the consultant is to see that the problems people are having in getting their jobs done are adequately addressed. Therefore, the consultant continues to ask, "Am I speaking with the right people?" and "How will this information be useful?"

All consulting requires follow-up to ensure meaningful organizational payoffs, and an understanding of the importance of follow-up should be arranged in advance with the client organization. Periodic reviews and reassessments are necessary, with alterations where appropriate, together with renewed commitments from both the client and the consultant. The effective consultant monitors follow-up activities to assure that the consulting endeavor produces successful consequences both for the client organization and for the consultant.

A final caveat

When working within a collaborative framework, the consultant needs to continually clarify the expectations of the chief executive and other members of the client organization. The definition of "consultant as expert" is so widespread within this culture that even though the consultant may have been completely clear during initial conversations with all parties, traditional expectations often surface anew during the consultation. Therefore, a consultant who wishes to work collaboratively with clients must understand that clarifying the client's expectations is a continuous responsibility.

References

Argyris, C. *Intervention theory and method.* Reading,
 Mass.: Addison-Wesley, 1970.

A small company president talks back to consultants.
 INC., 1980, *2* (May), 82-90.

Maier, N.R.F. *Psychology in industrial organizations.*
 Boston: Houghton Mifflin, 1973.

Miles, M. B., & Schmuck, R. A. The nature of organiza-
 tional development. In R. A. Schmuck & M. B. Miles
 (Eds.), *Organizational development in schools.* La Jolla,
 CA: University Associates, 1976. Pp. 2-3 and 7-10.

Nadler, D. A. *Feedback and organization development:
 using data-based methods.* Reading, MA: Addison-
 Wesley, 1977.

Steele F. *Consulting for organizational change.* Amherst,
 MA: University of Massachusetts Press, 1975.

What Is This Thing Called "Help"?

Arthur M. Freedman

There are at least four discernible functions which can be performed while attempting to manage or resolve one's own or another person's interpsychic or interpersonal "problems"—one might, however, choose to define these. Such functions might be referred to as "behaviors that are intended to be helpful."

STYLE I.   **Describing** another person's observable behavior
What is the other person saying and doing? How is the other person doing and saying these things?

STYLE II.   **Disclosing** one's own thoughts and feelings about the other's behavior
As you observe and take note of the other person's behavior, what feelings do you experience and what thoughts occur to you that relate to the other person's behaviors? How do the other person's actions affect you?

STYLE III. **Diagnosing or interpreting** hidden, non-observable motives or internal conflicts
What motives seem to lie, unseen, below the other person's surface behavior? What seems to be wrong with the other person? Does the other person seem to be trying to resolve some long-standing internal conflict in an inappropriate manner? Does he or she seem to act as though you were a different person from the person you really are?

STYLE V.   **Prescribing or recommending** specific remedies or action alternatives to be undertaken by the person with the "problem"
What do you think the other person should do to overcome the problem he or she says (or you think) he or she has?

Just about all of us have either directly experienced each of these intended styles of helping or recognize their possible use.

In practice, however, most people tend to rely almost exclusively on the **diagnosing/interpreting** or **pre-scribing/recommending** styles and underuse both the describing and **disclosing** styles.

I am convinced that this observed tendency on the part of professional or para-professional helpers is not only dysfunctional, but one that should be reversed. That is, **describing** and **disclosing** should become the primary styles employed by would-be helpers, and problem solvers should either de-emphasize or, preferably, discontinue the **diagnosing** and **prescribing** styles. My reasoning has been influenced by the following considerations.

Basic, significant information about how Smith's behaviors affect Brown is unexpressed and, therefore, withheld from Smith. Thus, the nature of the impact that Smith's actions have on Brown can only be implied from what Brown does after Smith has acted. Smith, in effect, lacks the opportunity to know just what feelings and thoughts Brown experiences after Smith acts. Such information could serve as a foundation for Smith to perform the **diagnosing** and **prescribing** functions for and by her or himself.

The recipient of **diagnostic** or **prescriptive** types of "helpful feedback" has little, if any, *ownership* of the information given because he or she did not contribute to its creation. Instead, the provider owns the feedback and probably has an emotional investment in making sure the recipient sees how "useful" the help is. In response to such "help," the recipient often *resists*. This usually takes the form of attempts to "help" the provider see and understand that the help offered is inappropriate and unlikely to be effective.

In **diagnosing** and **prescribing** the provider often assumes that he or she can know what would be functional and relevant for the recipient to know about and the most effective actions for the recipient to take. This attitude is highly presumptuous.

Even in those cases in which the **diagnosis** may be quite correct and the **prescriptions** may be effective, the helper must remember that the task in *truly* helping another person is *not* to give the recipient answers. Rather, help consists of providing the recipient with *access* to the knowledge and skills (the "tools") needed to analyze his or her own social, interpersonal, or internal problems and then to develop his or her own plan of action to deal with those problems.

The idea is not for the provider to solve one problem after another for the recipient, but, instead, to help that person learn to manage both present and *future* problems without outside help—not just those problems that currently concern the recipient.

When one person tries to tell what another person thinks and feels and then prescribe what the other ought to do about it all, the chances are that the provider is saying what would be true if he or she were in the recipient's position.

Only the recipient, however, is in the recipient's position. No one other than the recipient can ever fully know and appreciate the recipient's unique situation and concerns. Because of this, the provider depends upon the recipient.

When the provider **diagnoses** and/or **prescribes** and the recipient accepts what the provider is saying as valid and useful, then neither the recipient nor the provider are probably willing to assume responsibility for their own behavior. More likely, they each work out their own concerns through the other person and they each allow themselves to believe they have no personal responsibility for what is taking place. Thus, when things don't work out, each avoids "blame," but in different ways. For example, the provider can claim that the recipient just did not do everything that was **prescribed** or else did so incorrectly. The recipient can convince her or himself that the provider made an incorrect analysis and gave ineffective advice. If things do work out as a result of the recipient's effective implementation of the prescription, the recipient often *disowns* her or his *success*. A person cannot *earn* pride and self-esteem merely by carrying out someone else's prescription for managing one's own problems.

Finally, to the extent that the provider is effective in getting the recipient to accept the provider's **diagnosis** and/or **prescription**, the recipient does not have an opportunity to experiment with and practice his or her own, self-generated problem-solving skills. Such opportunities offer recipients a "stretching" or personal-growth experience. This could lead to the acquisition of new strengths (*competence* and *proficiency* in the use of practical skills). In turn, such acquisitions often constitute a basis for persons to begin to change their image of themselves (from being helpless, ineffectual, and dependent on stronger people to being more self-sufficient and able to manage more independently).

What purpose is served through the perpetuation of this dysfunctional tendency of would-be helpers to overuse the **diagnosing** and **prescribing** styles? Someone must derive benefits—or else so many of us would not use such styles so often. What is gained and/or avoided? Is there anything to prevent us from letting such tactics atrophy and eventually disappear— for example, as a result of not using them, not responding to them when another person uses them, rejecting another person's invitation to participate in their use, and withholding approval and acceptance of those of us who use them. I think some "restraining forces" discourage people from discontinuing the **diagnosing** and **prescribing** styles.

To **describe** and **disclose** oneself in the form of personal and open feedback to another person makes the

provider vulnerable to "attack" (rejection, criticism, or disapproval) from the recipient of such feedback and any witnesses to the transaction. People who give this kind of **descriptive** or (self-) **disclosing** feedback take a high risk.

For a would-be helper, to provide mostly **diagnoses** or **prescriptions** often seems more "economical" than **describing** or **disclosing** in terms of the amount of time the provider spends with the recipient. The provider obviously needs more time to help the recipient come to his or her own conclusions and then figure out what, if anything, he or she might wish to do than to merely tell the recipient what the provider thinks is happening and should be done.

The **diagnosing** and **prescribing** styles of help correspond more or less to our culture's accepted and sanctioned definition of "help." This model is established by the patient-physician relationship. That is, a sick person's responsibility for his or her condition ends when the person presents her or himself to the **diagnostic** and **prescriptive** (curative) expertise of the physician. Emotional difficulties and behavioral problems (in family, social, or work situations), however, are not "illnesses," and competent therapists and OD consultants are not necessarily physicians.

And most fundamental of all, most people who seek help from others—professionally or informally—tend not to consciously recognize that they have the power to perform the **diagnostic** and **prescriptive** functions for and by themselves when they have obtained sufficient amounts of authentic **descriptive** and **disclosing** feedback from concerned and committed peers.

What can be done to overcome these restraining forces?

1. As a provider of help, act counter to culturally communicated expectations and sanctioned tactics. Take risks inherent in **describing** and **disclosing** and refrain from making **diagnoses** and **prescriptions**.

2. As a provider of help, allow the recipient the courtesy and opportunity to experiment and practice with making his or her own **diagnoses** and **prescriptions**. Do not presume to believe that anyone but the provider is capable of performing these latter functions.

3. Take the time that is necessary to provide complete and authentic **descriptive** and **disclosing** feedback.

In summary, help can result in positive outcomes if

1. The provider (a) **describes** his or her perceptions of the recipient's observable behavior, and (b) **discloses** his or her feelings and thoughts about the recipient's observed behavior—including, if possible, any implications which all this might have for the provider.

2. The recipient performs (a) the **diagnostic**, analytic, and interpretive as well as (b) the **prescriptive** functions—perhaps using the provider as a "reality tester."

Consultation

Everyone at times needs help and everyone at times attempts to give help. Thus, in a sense, everyone is a consultant, since consultation is essentially a helping relationship. Consultation, however, cannot be effective unless and until help is perceived as helpful by the recipient, regardless of the helper's good intentions.

A consultant may offer help in many ways. To quote Curtis Mial's analogy: "The consultant may serve as exhaust valve, enabling the client to let off steam; as the ignition to spark action; as the accelerator to build up momentum; as the brake for too quick action; as the radiator absorbing some of the heat of controversy; as the shock absorbers when the going is rough; or as the fog lamps when the future is hazy. The consultant may fulfill a variety of functions, but one thing he [or she] is not: the driver." The consultant's responsibility is to help the client

- see the situation fully and realistically,
- consider alternative solutions to the problem,
- find and use appropriate resources,
- make the most of potential ability.

Definition

Consultation is a helping process emerging from a personal relationship established between one or more persons trying to solve a problem or develop a plan (the client) and one or more persons trying to help in these efforts (the consultant).

Consultative relationship

An effective consultative relationship is a shared quest requiring certain kinds of knowledge, attitudes, and skills of both parties. These attributes must be recognized and provided, and they depend upon the nature of the problem to be solved or action to be taken and on the duration and direction of the relationship.

Characteristics. The relationship may be characterized as
— *voluntary*, for the client trusts the consultant and is willing to maintain the relationship;

— *temporary*, for the relationship is understood as focusing on a particular problem or plan and as terminating on its solution or enactment;

— *supportive*, for the consultant focuses her help more on the support of the client than on the solution of the problem; and

— *disciplined*, for both the consultant and the client recognize the need for clear working standards and their mutual responsibility to maintain them.

Consultative process

An effective consultative process is essentially a data-gathering enterprise in which problems are defined and plans developed on the basis of the best appraisal of all available data.
Functions. The basic consultative functions are

— *reflective* toward the collection of data, by which the consultant helps the client see the situation surrounding the problem and identify his feelings about the situation;

— *diagnostic* toward the interpretation of data, by which the consultant helps the client analyze implications of the data thus gathered by examining the situation, exploring his feelings about it, and reassessing the stated problem; and

— *suggestive* toward the response to the data, by which the consultant helps the client develop an appropriate plan of action to deal effectively with the problem.

Consultative role

The role of the consultant requires functions common to other leadership roles, but it differs

— from the supervisory role in that the consultant is not directly responsible for the work of the client or for the outcome of the consultation;

— from the counseling role in that the consultant focuses on a problem or plan related to the client's particular leadership responsibilities; and

— from the training role in that the consultant functions within the context of an actual rather than a practice situation.

Qualifications. The consultant may be described as one who is

— wanted (one who is sought after for help);
— helpful (one who helps others to help themselves);
— informed (one who has a broad knowledge of the problem area);

— objective (one who has an unbiased point of view);
— trained (one who has specialized skill as a consultant);
— supportive (one who focuses more on the person than the problem);
— "unconflicted" (one whose advice may be either accepted or rejected);
— available (one who has adequate time for the task).

Consultative concerns

One social scientist, after scanning reports of consultation experiences, identified the following areas of concern as common threads:

— entry (entering—and re-entering—the client system and how the form and nature of entry predetermines certain consequences in the ensuing relationship);

— diagnosis (examination of motives of the client and the consultant, of problem definition and assessment of barriers);

— data collection (agreements upon kinds of data to be gathered and methods for gathering them);

— relationship (creating people relations, mutual acceptance of personal and resource worth);

— boundary definition (agreements about boundaries in the relationships and the roles taken);

— resource development (determining the areas in which the consultant can and should be a resource and how these resources may develop within the client system);

— decision making (how decisions will be made and what role consultants play in this process);

— termination (how relationships may be altered as they progress and are finally terminated without undue trauma to the system).

Consultative dilemmas

Certain stresses are inherent in the nature of consultation that cannot be removed without destroying the relationship. The ill effects of these difficulties, however, can be minimized by the consultant who is aware of their implications.

Authority Factor. The consultant always enters a consultative relationship as a person with authority derived either from the position in the organization or from possession of specialized knowledge. The emer-

gence of this added authority and power into the midst of a delicately balanced and intricate system of human relationships can cause suspicion, uncertainty, resentment, and conflict.

Intrusion of an Outsider. The consultant is by definition an outsider. Consequently, the insiders may feel that he or she does not understand their specific problem and its unique implications, although they may recognize the consultant as an expert on the problem in general.

Threat of an Expert. The help that a consultant in a specialized field can render is limited by the very fact of her expertness. Her presence implies that the resources and competence to solve the problem at hand are not available among members of the client group.

Conflict in Roles. The roles and attendant responsibilities of both consultant and client, when unclear and undefined, may produce differing expectations and make each unable to predict what the other will do. Frustration and wasted energies can result.

Resistance to Change. The consultant can expect either inertia or active resistance from the client whenever a change in the status quo is contemplated. Such resistance may be caused by fear of the unknown, threat to position, or fear of failure. Counterbalancing this resistance, however, are curiosity, interest, and the tendency of experiment.

Dependency. Some clients may prefer the consultant to tell them what to do rather than to think through the problem for themselves; others may resist help offered by the consultant. These tendencies toward dependence and counterdependence are to be expected in the development of any mature relationship.

Compulsive Action. The consultant may feel the need to demonstrate his or her value; the client may feel the need to arrive at a quick solution. Both may forget that quick results can jeopardize long-range goals.

Client Insecurity. The client may find it difficult to ask for help. He may be threatened by the suggestion that he needs help; unaware or reluctant to admit his own part in the problem; looking for assurance and sympathy more than for help in seeing the problem clearly and realistically; and resentful of the help offered or the helper.

Consultant Objectivity. The consultant, especially under the pressure of dependency or resistance, needs to be aware of and sensitive to the possibilities of exploiting the consultative relationship to meet his or her needs, for success, reward, approval, friendship, or whatever.

Client Motivation. The consultant must be aware of the range of possible motivations in the client: the need for justifying a preferred solution or course of action; the need for avoidance of responsibility for final action; the need for expressing dissatisfaction by a legitimate means.

Disengagement. One of the consultant's goals is to work her- or himself out of a job. Both the consultant and the client may resist terminating the relationship. The client may find security in leaning on the consultant; the consultant may enjoy being needed.

Process Intervention: An Operational Philosophy*

ARTHUR M. FREEDMAN

During a "shadow" consulting assignment, I observed and coached two internal organizational development consultants as they worked with the staff of a treatment program in a mental health facility. During a lunch break, while we analyzed the morning's events, I asked the two consultants for some feedback on the interventions I had made with the client group.

The consultants responded that my interventions seemed helpful, but wondered whether, by making them, I was implying that the consultants did something wrong. They asked if I was making the interventions that they should have made. The consultants acknowledged that often they did not feel sure when to make what kinds of interventions, how often, or about which issues.

This led to a discussion of our shared uncertainties and insecurity regarding our own OD skills and knowledge. How could any of us always know the best moment at which to intervene effectively during a process consultation? The appropriate moment for a particular intervention may come and go without either consultant or client realizing it.

These same colleagues helped me to articulate an operational "philosophy" of making interventions which, until then, had existed only implicitly.

An operational philosophy

I divide process interventions into three distinct classes: conceptual inputs, coaching, and process observations. Each can be considered in terms of (a) what it might look or sound like when it is made; (b) the objective(s) which it can facilitate; (c) when it can be made; and (d) the form or style it might take.

Conceptual inputs

An example of a conceptual input might sound like this:

Member A to the client group: I am beginning to see that you people get pretty upset when I discuss the

*I am grateful to Drs. Irvin Roth and Franklin Weingarten for inspiring this paper.

© 1983 NTL Institute

work I want you to do. I can see that when you get upset, the work doesn't get done as well or as fast as I think it should. But what I don't know is what do I do that gets you all so upset? Maybe I need to hear a little of what these people [the OD consultants] call "feedback."

Member E to Member A: Well, I guess I could give you some feedback. You know, you can be pretty overbearing sometimes, and some of these new people don't know how to handle you.

[pause]

Member A to Member E: What the hell are you talking about? What's that supposed to mean?

Consultant to the client group: It seems to me that we're experimenting with the idea of giving each other some feedback on how we perceive and react to each other's behavior, but we're running into a problem. Just what is feedback? And how do you give it so the person [stating the problem] who is getting it can use it? Does that sound right to you? [double checking for agreement or disagreement]

[Client group indicates agreement by nodding their heads and saying yes.]

Consultant to client group: Okay. Maybe it would help if I laid out some ground rules for giving feedback. [More nonverbal affirmation from the client group.] For me, useful feedback has three parts, and if any part is left out, the value of the feedback decreases: First, describe what the other person is saying and doing that concerns you; second, describe what you feel when you focus your attention on the other person's actions; third, describe what you are most likely to do in response to the other person's actions—that is, describe the implications. An example of complete feedback would be this: "I noticed a moment ago that you reached over and patted me on the back when I commented on Bill's idea. And when I turned around to look at you, you were smiling. [description of the focal behavior] I felt pretty good—as if you were saying you thought I was saying the right thing. I like that because

I need some reassurance...and, I felt you approved of my ideas. [expression of feelings] Now I'll probably be a more active participant at these meetings. I don't think I'll hold myself back so much." [statement of implications]

Member E to Member A: Yeah. That helps me to organize my thoughts better. What I was trying to say to you was that when you come over to us when we're working, you seem to see yourself as trying to "discuss" our work with us. But from my point of view, you come across as a critic.

Consultant to Member E: Can you say what it is that he says or does that gives you the impression of him as a critic? [coaching]

Member E to Member A: Yes. You never tell us that we're doing okay. All I can remember you saying are things like how you would approach the problem a different way than the way we'd already done it. [description of behavior] And when you say things like that, I just want to hide somewhere and get out of the way. [close to expression of feelings] So, sometimes I change the subject if I can or I "remember" another appointment I have to get away from you. Naturally, the work stops. [statement of implications]

The objective of a conceptual input process intervention is to provide members of a client group with an organizing principle that can help them see clearly the distinctions between typical, but not optimal, behavior—i.e., the things people say and do and the style with which they say and do them—and more effective behavior. Since conceptual inputs tend to be easily remembered, they can be referred to in the future. When a consultant intervenes in this way, he or she provides clients with a new vocabulary and conceptual system that is quite explicit and that is shared and understood by all the client-group members. This new vocabulary avoids confusion and misunderstandings because the clients are likely to remember, understand, and use the behaviors to which the new "language" refers.

One can use conceptual input interventions at any time during a process consultation, as long as the contract between the consultant and the client group allows this kind of consultant behavior. The best time to make a conceptual input intervention is immediately after a transaction has occurred between members that clearly illustrates the undesirable consequences of inappropriate or ineffective behavior. Note that in the above exchange the consultant timed the intervention to "piggy-back" on Member A's expressed confusion (an unproductive human experience). This is when the intervention is most likely to make sense to the client-group members. When people understand the relevance of an intervention, they will most likely use it.

A conceptual input should be succinct. And, just as

important, it should be comprehensible to the members of the client group. Making the perfectly appropriate intervention at exactly the right time does no good if the consultant chooses terms so academic and esoteric that the people can't understand what was said. This style cause clients to write the consultant off as an irrelevant, ivory-tower type.

Coaching

An example of facilitating the acquisition of desirable, functional habits of interacting might sound like this:

[following a conceptual input on feedback]

Member A to Member B: I think you act in an arbitrary manner. [A is labeling B.]

Consultant to Member A: What is it about Member B's behavior that has led you to conclude that she is "arbitrary?" [an invitation to focus on observable behavior rather than using abstract labels]

Member A to Member B: You sometimes ask us for information to help you make decisions. But after you get it, even if you say you appreciate our ideas, you don't seem to use them. [description of behavior] The way you act suggests to me that you never really wanted our ideas and that you were just going through a formality. It's as if you knew that you would stick to your original decision regardless of what we might say. [conjecture]

Consultant to Member B: How do you feel about what A just said? [inviting B to share her feelings with A]

Member B to Member A: I am confused and wonder whether anything I say to you has any meaning or significance. It's as if I was being disregarded and held off at a distance when I really want to get close to you and work with you. I guess I feel pretty disappointed. Now I'm not sure if I'll bother giving you any information the next time you ask for it. I probably won't. I don't see what value it would have. You'd probably just put me down again by disregarding what I say. [an expression of feelings as well as a statement of implications]

Member A to Member B: What you say helps me to make some sense out of what has been happening between us over the last several weeks. I recognize now that there's been some tension, but I just pretended that it didn't mean anything. Now I don't know quite what to do about it. [an acknowledgment of the feedback and of having reached an impasse—this implies the possibility that A might want help in identifying some functional alternatives for dealing with the problem, but she is not expressing this.]

Consultant to Member A: Would you be interested in hearing if anyone else in the group has some ideas about what we can do about this problem? [a test of whether A is willing to assume responsibility for seeking new alternatives]

Member A to Consultant: I'm feeling a need to think about this for a while. It has a lot of implications, and I'm not yet ready to share them all with anyone else. Right now I want some quiet time alone. I'll check back with the rest of you after I've had a chance to mull it over. [acknowledging her desire to disengage, temporarily, with an option to reopen the issue later]

The objective of a coaching intervention is to assist members of a client group to practice using new behaviors with which they want to become proficient. Coaching interventions are most effectively made either during the early, standard-setting phases of the consultative process—when they can "shape" the kinds and sequence of interpersonal communications early—or right after a conceptual input has been made that serves as a basis of the coaching effort. In either instance, the coaching interventions should be discontinued as soon as the client group's members demonstrate they can employ the new behaviors without assistance or when some members begin systematically to perform this coaching function for each other.

Coaching interventions, like conceptual inputs, should be brief and to the point. They should invite participants to experiment with new behavior, not reprimand or coerce them.

Process observations

A process observation might sound like this:

Member C to the client group: A little while ago I wanted to share an observation with the rest of you which I thought might have been useful at the time, but I restrained myself. I wanted to say we've been on this topic for 20 minutes without coming to a conclusion. You're wasting my time. You aren't accomplishing anything. You ought to move on to a different issue. [a task-related function] I guess I was afraid that I would alienate myself from the rest of you by doing something "unpopular." [expression of feelings]

Consultant to Member C: If I hear you accurately, you seem to be saying that you're reluctant to perform a task or maintenance function for the group even though you think it is needed because it might be unpopular. And that means you'd be risking the possibility of getting alienated from the rest of the group.

[paraphrasing] Am I right? [double checking]

Member C to Consultant: That's about it.

Consultant to Member C: An additional issue might be the style or the manner in which you were thinking of performing that function. By saying it the way you just did, you probably would have given me a basis for feeling bad about myself. As if I had done something wrong. And that might have led to my wanting to hurt you or put you down or cut you off. [hypothetical personal feedback] But now I wonder if you can think of a different style of saying the same thing. Can you find a new way which is less likely to result in your feeling cut out of the group? [an invitation to consider and experiment with an alternative form of performing needed task or maintenance functions]

Member C to the client group: Yes. I think so. Let me know how this comes across. It seems to me that we've been going over the same points several times now. It's kind of like we've been recycling. [description of group behavior] And I'm finding myself feeling unproductive. And that leaves me pretty impatient. Has anyone else felt that way? If so, what do we want to do about it? [Considerably more self-disclosure and ownership of the speaker's ideas and feelings are publicly expressed here; also, instead of a critical and punitive demand being made of the other members of the client group, C includes himself as a part of the problem and invites the rest of the group to collaborate in dealing with it. This is action being taken on the basis of the person's observations and feelings; it carries the idea of implications one step forward out of the hypothetical and into reality.]

Another example of a process observation is this:

Consultant to the client group: I've noticed that we've spent a lot of time jumping from one issue to another without seeming to finish up any of them. For example, Sam raised the question about whether or not we, as a group, wanted to spend our time giving each other feedback. Then Toni pointed out we could give one person feedback at a time in a way that would enable the receiver to decide whether he or she wanted to renegotiate some interpersonal contracts with the givers. In making this point, Toni seemed to redirect the group's attention away from Sam. A kind of a topic jump about which Sam did not do anything. Then, before the group responded to Toni's idea, Joe stated that he thought we ought to focus on some of the things that happened three days ago during the general session which he thought were getting us hung up this afternoon—another topic jump. [a demonstration of the tracking or summarizing task function]

This indicates to me that we're having trouble figuring out how we can make group decisions about what we're going to do with our time. [spelling out the apparent problem confronting the group] Now I'm uncertain about just what's going on and a bit impatient [expression of feelings] for a clear, explicit group decision. Just what is it that we would like to do? [statement of expectations and a direct request to the client-group members to disclose their opinions acting on implications]

The objectives of a process observation intervention include the following:

1. Heightening the client-group members' awareness of the significance of the distinction between the content and process dimensions of transactions occurring within a group. In the example above, the consultant illustrated both what kinds of topics or issues the group was working on (the "content") and how the group seemed to be operating—that is, topic jumping and absence of explicit, group-level decision making (the "process").

2. Increasing the group's awareness of the implications and consequences of its members' actions—for example, how an individual's behavior may contribute to the creation or continuation of normative standards (both functional and dysfunctional) governing group members' behaviors. In the example above, Toni's topic jump might have contributed to the creation of a group norm that implies that, in this group, it is okay to change topics and cut off another person. When Joe interrupted Toni, another contribution might have been made to the continuation of that norm. A process observation can also be used to highlight implications and consequences by pointing out how the group is affected by the failure to perform needed task and maintenance functions or what happens when it employs different group decision-making procedures.

3. Providing an observable model of functional behaviors that demonstrates how one can facilitate a group's movement in the direction of its objectives. In the first example above, the consultant modeled many functional activities, including paraphrasing, double checking, personal feedback, and helping another person experiment with new ways of behaving. In the second example, the consultant modeled tracking by summarizing, stating the issue, expressing feelings and expectations, and asking for opinions and information.

Process observation interventions have the greatest effect during the early phases of the consultation. After any process observation is modeled once or twice, the consultant should refrain from making these interventions. This gives client-group members more opportunities to experiment with and practice performing these facilitative functions. To the extent they do this, they can acquire increased self-sufficiency. This tends to preclude their becoming dependent on the "expert" consultant to perform such functions. If the client-group members do not assume responsibility for performing these functions after they have been modeled once or twice, the consultant might keep track of the implications and

consequences of their not having been performed. Then, during a "stop action" or some other designated process session, these could be reported to the group along with a question: "What, if anything, do we want to do about this situation?" This explicitly invites and allows the clients to negotiate a contract among themselves to ensure that needed functions are performed when they are most relevant and to avoid the unnecessary, undesired consequences of failing to perform the functions.

Process observations usually take a bit longer than other types of interventions. The consultant attempts to illustrate constantly shifting group processes in sufficient detail to help the client-group members not only see what is happening right now, but also to do the same thing themselves in the future.

In conclusion, I am reminded of Saul Alinsky's "iron rule": "Don't ever do anything for anyone that they can do for themselves." If one or more client-group members has the skills and knowledge to perform necessary group functions, he or she is entitled to opportunities to put such skill and knowledge into practical use. Too much assistance on the part of the OD consultant leads to stultification, dependency, and indifference.

Dimensions of the Consultant's Job*

Ronald Lippitt

Consultation, like supervision is a general label for many variations of relationship. The general definition of consultation used in this paper assumes that:

1. the consultation relationship is a *voluntary relationship between*
2. *a professional helper* (consultant) and *help-needing system* (client)
3. in which the consultant is attempting to *give help* to the client in the solving of some current or potential *problem*,
4. and the relationship is perceived as *temporary* by both parties..
5. Also, the consultant is an *"outsider,"* i.e., not a part of any hierarchical power system in which the client is located.

Some additional clarification of this condensed definition is needed. The client is conceived to be any functioning social unit, such as a family, industrial organization, individual, committee, staff, membership association, governmental department, delinquent gang, or hospital staff. The consultant is usually a professional helper, such as a marriage counselor, management consultant, community organizer, minister, social worker, human relations trainer, psychiatrist, applied anthropologist, group therapist, or social psychologist. The role of psychological "outsider" may sometimes be taken by a consultant located within the client system, such as a member of the personnel department.

This article does not consider consultation with the single individual as client. This relationship has been explored extensively in the literature on counseling and psychotherapy. The focus of this article is on the group or larger social system as client.

The larger social system as client

One way of examining the role of the consultant is in terms of the series of questions or problems the consultant must pose for her- or himself and work on during the course of a consulting relationship. Each of these questions can be viewed as a professional problem on which

*Reprinted from *The Journal of Social Issues*, 1959, *15*(2), 5-12.

information is needed, about which theorizing must be done, action must be taken, and feedback must be sought by the consultant in order to get data about the consequences of the helping actions. The sequence of the questions formulated below does not represent any assumption that this is the orderly flow of questions and problems in the carrying through of a consultation relationship. Many of the questions are being worked on simultaneously at any one time and the questions keep recurring as the process of consultation unfolds. But to formulate them as dimensions of a consultant's role, we need to examine them one by one, rather than try to reproduce the multidimensional complexity of the consultant's job as he or she experiences it at any moment in time.

Question I: What seems to be the difficulty? Where does it come from? What's maintaining it?

Every consultant has a cluster of ideas, or a set of concepts, which guide her or his perception of "what exists" and "what is going on" when he or she comes in contact with a particular organization or social unit. This cluster of ideas is the consultant's theory about the nature of groups and what makes them behave the way they do. For some consultants, the theory may be largely inarticulated, and the concepts may not have much systematic relationship to each other. Nevertheless, the consultant must have some kind of theory so as to determine "what to see" and "how to understand" when he or she views the complexities of group or organizational life. Other consultants approach their task with a relatively systematic conceptual framework, such as psychoanalytic theory, structure-function theory, learning theory, social-conflict theory, or role theory. Those without theoretical background have a harder time organizing and comprehending what they see. Those with a more systematic theory have a harder time noticing and interpreting important events which are not taken into account by their theory.

In addition to having a systematic descriptive-analytic theory, the consultant must have a diagnostic theory which guides her or him in focusing on symptoms of pain or disruption in the system and on evidence that things are not "normal" or "healthy." Usually a diagnostic theory includes both ideas about symptoms and concepts about the basic causes of certain symptoms. In our study of a wide variety of consultants (Lippitt, Watson and Westley, 1958), it seemed possible to delineate several typical diagnostic orientations:

1. An inappropriate distribution of power, too diffuse or too centralized.
2. Blockage and immobilization of productive energy.
3. Lack of communication between the subparts of a system.
4. A lack of correspondence between external reality and the situation as perceived by the client.
5. A lack of clarity or commitment to goals for action.
6. A lack of decision-making and action-taking skills.

These and other theories about "the source of trouble" provide the basis for selective probing to secure information from the client which will be used to interpret the nature of the difficulty and to make decisions about what type of helping should be tried. Also, such a diagnostic theory helps to define the directions along which improvement is desired and expected and, therefore, defines the symptoms of improvement which the consultant will watch for to know whether there are desired consequences of the helping efforts.

Because these two frameworks of theory, systematic and diagnostic, play such a central role in the nature and quality of the performance of the consultant, it would seem particularly important for research to explore the use in practice of systematic theory and the development of improved diagnostic theory. One of the most unexplored areas is that of the exact nature of the relationship between general systematic theory about groups and organizations and diagnostic theory about pathology of social systems.

Question II: What are my motives as a consultant for becoming involved in this helping relationship? What are the bases of my desire to promote change?

Being a *professional* helper implies responsibility for a high level of self-awareness about one's own values and needs as they may influence the helping relationship. Some critical observers of the American scene think we demonstrate the value that "any change is better than no change." Such a value would relieve both consultants and clients of a great deal of responsibility for goal setting and would make it easy to label all resistance to change as bad. Clearly, such a position is untenable. Another extreme position maintains that any planned efforts to stimulate change in others is manipulative and undemocratic. Very little significant work would get done in the world if this unrealistic idea prevailed. The observation of any meaningful social process reveals continuous efforts of people and groups to influence each other in the interest of various types of goals. The consultant must clarify her own particular goals and motivations for influencing others.

Even in the field of individual psychotherapy a large proportion of the individuals in need of help do not, for various reasons, take the initiative to seek help. And if one individual or subgroup from the potential client approaches a consultant for help, can this be considered as a request for help from the total system?

This initiative problem means that consultants who work with groups must be prepared to stimulate and develop helping relationships. This requires thoughtfully clarifying values involved in such "intervention" into the ongoing life of a group. Various consultants have formulated different bases for "the right to intervene" with attempts to give help.

1. Some consultants think that a group is "calling for help" when there is evidence that the social processes of the group are causing individual suffering, such as rejection, isolation, scapegoating. Individual discomfort and frustration of group members is taken as a valid basis for the judgment that "something needs to be done."

2. Other consultants tend to take a "group welfare" orientation and perceive a basis for intervention when there are symptoms that the groups' efforts are inefficient and inadequate to move toward its goals.

3. Other consultants may take an "institutional welfare" orientation and evaluate a group as warranting intervention if its efforts cause disruption or "pain" for the larger organization or for neighboring groups, such as breakdown in one department of an organization or disruption of the neighborhood life by a delinquent gang.

In addition to the "justification for intervention," there is the question of "what goals for change." On the basis of diagnostic observations, does the consultant formulate goals for change in the client or does she work only in terms of goals formulated by the client? Some consultants act only in terms of goals which have been collaboratively formulated and accepted by both the client and the consultant. Other consultants think they have a right to certain methodological goals, such as using good procedures for problem solving, but have no right to take positions on the answers to the problems.

Question III: What seem to be the present, or potential, motivations of the client toward change and against change?

The analysis of change forces and resistance forces is an important part of the consultant's initial assessment and also a continuing challenge during all stages of the consulting relationship. A conceptual framework for analyzing these forces has been presented by Lewin (1947), by Coch and French (1948), and by Lippitt, Watson, and Westley (1958). Our comments here are limited to a few special aspects of the motivational situation in working with groups as clients.

In work with individuals, feelings of pain and dissatisfaction with the present situation are most frequently the dominant driving forces for change, but in work with groups very often one of the most important motivations is a desire to improve group efficiency, to achieve some higher level of functioning, even though there may be no critical problems in the present situation. Therefore, one of the consultant's jobs with groups is to help clarify "images of potentiality" rather than to focus on ways of alleviating present pain. Perhaps the most crucial aspect of motivational analysis in working with groups is the study of the nature and effects of the interdependence between the subparts (e.g., subgroups or departments) in the client system. One subgroup's eagerness to change may not reflect readiness for change of other subgroups or of the total organization. Learning about the supporting and conflicting relationships between subgroups is a crucial task, and success in getting these facts will determine to a great degree whether the consultant is able to develop the necessary and appropriate relationship to the total group and to its various subparts. One of the most frequent forms of resistance to change in group clients is the perception by certain subgroups that the consultant is more closely related to other subgroups and is "on their side" in any conflict of interests.

Question IV: What are my resources as a consultant for giving the kind of help that seems to be needed now or that may develop later?

The requirements of time and skill needed to carry through a psychotherapeutic relationship with an individual have become fairly clear. Usually, the situation is not so clear in working out a consultative relationship with a group or organization. Quite frequently a consultant relationship with a group will require much more time and a greater variety of helping skills than are frequently in the consultation with social units than with individuals. Often the consultant offers diagnostic help and arrives at certain recommendations for improvement or change but offers no continuity in actually working through the meaning of the diagnostic findings for changing procedures, practices, and interaction patterns. This lack of continuity often results in disruption and demoralization because of the inadequacy of the client group to cope with the implications for change without further technical help from a consultant. As in medicine, the consultant who has the analytic skills for diagnosis does not have the training and therapeutic skills required for working through the implications of the diagnosis. A consultant team would seem to be the creative solution in many cases.

Question V: What preliminary steps are needed to explore and establish a consulting relationship?

As pointed out previously, groups as groups are much slower to develop and clarify an awareness of the need for help than are individuals. Therefore, group consultants have a greater responsibility for developing techniques of helping the social system develop this awareness through appropriate communication procedures. This often requires taking an active initiative of a kind frowned on in the field of individual consultation. Examples of useful techniques are presented by Lippitt, Watson, and Westley (1958).

A "trial period" or pilot project as a basis for exploring a possible consulting relationship should also be emphasized. This provides an opportunity to establish relationships with all the subgroups and to clarify expectations about readiness to change and about the nature of the consultant's role.

In initial contacts it is very difficult to know whether an administrator, for example, is speaking as a representative of the organization, as a representative of a small subgroup, or only for himself. The techniques of dual entry and multiple entry have been developed to meet this situation. Getting into contact with the "whole" client is one of the most challenging problems for the group consultant. In an organization or community this often means working closely with a group of representatives from all units to keep channels of communication open to all parts of the system.

Question VI: How do I as consultant guide, and adapt to, the different phases of the process of changing?

The consultant who works through the problems of changing with a group finds that there are several phases or stages and that those phases require different levels of relationship and different kinds of helping skills. Starting from Lewin's (1947) three-phase analysis, Lippitt, Watson, and Westley (1958) discovered in their comparative study of a population of consultants that seven phases could be identified with some degree of consistency:

1. developing a need for change;
2. establishing a consulting relationship;
3. clarifying the client problem;
4. examining alternative solutions and goals;
5. transforming intentions into actual change efforts;
6. generalizing and stabilizing a new level of functioning or group structure; and
7. achieving a terminal relationship with the consultant and a continuity of change-ability.

These are very general labels for a great variety of activities, but they do seem to clarify some of the shifts of goal and changes of consulting activity that take place during the total cycle of a consulting relationship.

As the consultant works with a group on examining alternative possibilities for improvement, it usually becomes clear that various types of special skill training will be needed to support the group's change efforts. Most consulting relationships with groups require a consultant-trainer role to carry through on problem solving. It is important for the consultant to clarify for herself the nature and timing of this shift from the more nondirective role of helping a group develop and clarify its own goals for change to the more active, directive role of helping the group learn the procedures and skills needed for them to move with efficiency toward the goals they have established. A group may flounder in its change efforts because the consultant has not been able to shift from the consultant role appropriate to the earlier phases of consultation to the more active training role which is usually necessary for carrying through the later phases of consultation.

Question VII: How do I help promote a continuity of creative change-ability?

A successful process of consultation with an organization or a group ends with at least three kinds of learnings:

1. The organization has learned to cope more adequately with the problem or problems which initiated the consulting process.

2. The organization has learned how to clarify future problems as they emerge and to make appropriate decisions about seeking outside help when needed.

3. The organization has learned new procedures and new types of organization to help it maintain a healthy state of change-ability in adapting to changing conditions and in utilizing potential for creative improvement in group functioning and productivity. Perhaps the most challenging task for the consultant in this regard is to discover ways of training the group to use procedures of data collection and analysis on a continuing basis which will permit the identification of new problems and possibilities. In small face-to-face groups, this may mean helping the group develop functions of group observation and feedback as a continuing part of the group practice, without continuing dependency on the consultant. In larger organizations it may mean helping in the collection, feedback, and skill training which will maintain the organization's continuous process of creative adaptation and social invention.

We have tried to emphasize some of the dimensions which represent a special challenge to consultants working with organizations or groups as contrasted to those working with individuals as clients. Perhaps the greatest challenge is that of continuously exploring the relevance of systematic theory from the behavioral sciences and finding opportunities for contributing to the body of theory through efforts to achieve a conceptual grasp of "what's going on," as we work at the job of giving help to groups in solving their problems of development and productivity. A basic integration of scientific theory and professional skills will be the continuing need as this field of social engineering develops.

References

Coch, L., & French, J.R.P., Jr. Overcoming resistance to change. *Human Relations*, 1948, *1*, 512-532.

Lewin, K. Frontier in group dynamics. *Human Relations*, 1947, *1*, 5-41.

Lippitt, R., Watson, J., & Westley, B. *The dynamics of planned change*. New York: Harcourt, Brace, 1958.

Some Skills in the Process of Stimulating Change

Skill area 1

The consultant assesses her or his personal motivations, and relationship to the "client." Here the term "consultant" may refer to an individual, a group, or an organization. Some abilities needed for this aspect of change include

- understanding the consultant's own motivation in seeing a need for change and wanting to bring about a change;

- understanding and working in terms of a philosophy and ethics of change;

- predicting the relation of one change to other possible changes, or to those that come later;

- determining the possible units of change:

  1. What seems to be needed?
  2. What is possible to the client?

- determining the size, character, and structural make-up of the clients;

- determining the barriers, the resistance, the degree of readiness to change;

- determining the resources available for overcoming barriers and resistance; and

- knowing how to determine the consultant's own strategic role in light of the situation and abilities.

Skill area 2

Helping clients become aware of the need for change and for the diagnostic process. Some abilities needed for this aspect of change include

- determining the level of sensitivity the clients have to the need for change;

- determining the methods which clients believe should be used in change;

- creating awareness of the need for considering change and diagnosis through shock, permissiveness, demonstration, research, guilt, and so forth;

- raising the client's aspirations and making aspirations realistic;

- creating a perception of the potential for change;

- establishing acceptance of a methodical plan whose use will require patience;

- identifying possible sources of help in this change;

- creating a feeling of responsibility to actively participate in the change process.

Note: Each of these skills may be pertinent to changing an individual, a person's relations with others, the relations among several others, a total group, a community, or widely held opinion. Any client becomes a consultant at some point in the normal development of the change process.

Skill area 3

Collaborative diagnosis by the consultant and client concerning the situation, behavior, understanding, feeling, or performance to be modified. Some abilities needed for this aspect of change include

- making catharsis possible and acceptable when indicated as a starting point;

- using diagnostic instruments appropriate to the problem: surveys, maps, score cards, observation;

- diagnosis in terms of causes rather than "goods" or "bads";

• helping clients to examine their own motivations;

• examining the relation of one change to other changes possible in that situation and helping clients understand;

• clarifying the interrelationship or roles between consultant and client; and

• dealing wisely and respectfully with the client's ideology, myths, traditions, and values.

Skill area 4

Deciding upon the problem; involving others in this decision; planning action; and practicing these plans. Some abilities needed include

• knowing techniques in arriving at a group decision;

• examining the consequences of possible decisions;

• making a step-wise plan;

• practicing plan implementation;

• providing for replanning and assessment at later stages;

• providing administrative organization; and

• eliciting and eliminating alternatives.

Skill area 5

Carrying out the plan successfully and productively. Some abilities needed for this aspect of change include

• building and maintaining the morale of the clients as they try the change;

• deciding upon the amount of action to be taken before assessment of progress and process being used;

• understanding the effects of stress on client's beliefs and behavior;

• defining objectives in a manner that leads to easy definition of methods; and

• creating a perception of the need for relating methods to the goal in mind.

Skill area 6

Evaluation and assessment of client's progress, methods of working, and human relations. Some abilities needed for this aspect of change include

• diagnosing causes of inefficient group action through the use of measuring instruments: interviews, interaction awareness panel; and

• using score cards, rating scales, and other instruments.

Skill area 7

Ensuring continuity, spread, maintenance, and transference of the change. Some abilities needed for this aspect of change include

• creating a perception of responsibility for participation in many persons;

• developing wide support for change;

• developing others' appreciation and support of participants' work.

Consultative Skills

The following list of attitudes and abilities are fundamental to the consultant's role of supporting the consultative relationship and implementing the helping process.

Listening. Diagnosing and understanding the thinking, motivations, and biases of the client both in presenting and in working on the problem. The consultant needs to hear the problem in terms of the client's attitudes and understandings without prejudging them.

Empathy. Identifying with the client's point of view makes real communication possible. The consultant may fail because of a basic lack of interest in or appreciation for the client.

Flexibility. Adjusting to the client's environment, terminology, habits, traditions, and ways of work. Adapting to a special circumstance or to the unexpected is essential if the consultant is to respond to the situation in which the problem exists.

Confidence. Recognizing and encouraging the client's potential to grow and learn from experience. Part of the consultative task is to create conditions in which the client not only solves the immediate problem but learns how to solve problems in the future.

Objectivity. Making a realistic analysis of the consultant's own attitudes, abilities, motivations, biases, and stereotypes as they relate to the particular relationship with a particular client. The consultant's own self-awareness is essential for guarding against advocating change for the sake of change, against encouraging dependence, against the temptation to act the expert outside of her or his own competence.

Mutuality. Developing real communication with the client to recognize shared interests, experiences, values, and standards as a basis for establishing the consultative relationship on a personal level.

Support. Entering the relationship as a shared quest with the client to assess and use the skills, knowledge, and experience of the client. The consultant needs to establish with the client mutual confidence in which the contributions of all can be used without concern for their source.

Experimentation. Maintaining a spirit of experimentation and exploration in the work on the problem combined with a sense of commitment to any one action step planned. Fundamental to the consultative process is the standard of constant evaluation, with information collected on the effectiveness of each action step and further steps planned on the basis of that data.

Timing. Asking questions, offering information, making suggestions at the moment that the client is ready to hear and respond. A sense of timing is fundamental to effective consultation at every level of the relationship and every point in the process.

An OD Consultant's Self-Assessment

I. Entry and Contract Building

Please complete the next two scales by circling one number on each.

A. I rate my *knowledge* right now on this topic as:

Lo		Md		Hi
1	2	3	4	5

B. I rate my *interest* right now on this topic as:

Lo		Md		Hi
1	2	3	4	5

II. Diagnosis

Diagnosis can be divided into a variety of topics. Here are some that I believe are important: (a) Goal clarity and agreement; (b) Communication patterns; (c) Leadership and influence; (d) Problem-solving capabilities; (e) Decision-making processes; (f) Types of conflict and interdependence, and (g) Role definitions and responsibilities.

Please complete each of the following five-point scales by printing a "K" to stand for how much knowledge you have now on the topic and an "I" to stand for your degree of interest right now on the topic.

A. Diagnosing goal clarity and agreement:

Lo		Md		Hi
1	2	3	4	5

B. Diagnosing communication patterns:

Lo		Md		Hi
1	2	3	4	5

C. Diagnosing leadership and influence:

Lo		Md		Hi
1	2	3	4	5

D. Diagnosing problem-solving capabilities:

Lo		Md		Hi
1	2	3	4	5

E. Diagnosing decision-making processes:

Lo		Md		Hi
1	2	3	4	5

F. Diagnosing types of conflict and interdependence:

Lo		Md		Hi
1	2	3	4	5

G. Diagnosing role definitions and responsibilities:

Lo		Md		Hi
1	2	3	4	5

H. Are there any other variables you'd like to learn to diagnose? (If yes, please list them here.)

III. Intervention

OD interventions can be classified into three basic categories: (a) Mode of intervention; (b) Focus of attention; (c) Diagnosed problems. The questions below are organized into these three categories.

A. Mode of Intervention

I rate my current knowledge (K) and interest (I) on each of the following modes of intervention as follows: (Print a "K" and an "I" on each of the following scales.)

1. Training (education)

Lo		Md		Hi
1	2	3	4	5

2. Process consultation (coaching)

Lo		Md		Hi
1	2	3	4	5

3. Confrontation

Lo		Md		Hi
1	2	3	4	5

4. Data feedback

Lo		Md		Hi
1	2	3	4	5

5. Problem solving

Lo		Md		Hi
1	2	3	4	5

6. Plan making

Lo		Md		Hi
1	2	3	4	5

7. OD task force establishment

Lo		Md		Hi
1	2	3	4	5

8. Techno-structural activity

Lo		Md		Hi
1	2	3	4	5

9. Are there any other modes of intervention you'd like to learn to use? (If yes, please list them here.)

B. *Focus on attention*

I rate my current knowledge (K) and interest (I) on each of the following intervention targets as follows: (Print a "K" and an "I" on each of the following scales.)

1. Total Organization (district or building)

Lo		Md		Hi
1	2	3	4	5

2. Intergroup (two or more)

Lo		Md		Hi
1	2	3	4	5

3. Team/Group

Lo		Md		Hi
1	2	3	4	5

4. Dyad/Triad

Lo		Md		Hi
1	2	3	4	5

5. Role

Lo		Md		Hi
1	2	3	4	5

6. Person

Lo		Md		Hi
1	2	3	4	5

7. Are there any other targets for intervention you'd like to learn more about? (If yes, please list them here.)

C. *Diagnosed problems*

I rate my current knowledge (K) and interest (I) on
intervening to solve each of these problems as follows:
(Print a "K" and an "I" on each of the following scales.)

1. Goal clarity and agreement

Lo		Md		Hi
1	2	3	4	5

2. Communication patterns

Lo		Md		Hi
1	2	3	4	5

3. Leadership and influence

Lo		Md		Hi
1	2	3	4	5

4. Problem-solving capabilities

Lo		Md		Hi
1	2	3	4	5

5. Decision-making processes

Lo		Md		Hi
1	2	3	4	5

6. Conflict and interdependence

Lo		Md		Hi
1	2	3	4	5

7. Role definitions and responsibilities

Lo		Md		Hi
1	2	3	4	5

8. Are there any other problems for intervention you'd
   like to learn more about? (If yes, please list them here.)

Pre-Lab Rating of Consultative and Change-Agent Concerns

ROBERT CHIN

The following areas of concern are common to most relationships between a consultant or a change-agent and her or his client system. In assessing your own strengths and weaknesses as a change-agent, how would you score yourself on each of these? Place a "Y" to indicate where you feel you are now and an "X" where you would realistically desire to move.

	Little Ability	Some	Moderate	Considerable	Great Ability
1. **Self-awareness** Aware of one's own personal needs that might be served in the client and/or consultant/client relationship.					
2. **Entry** Entering (and re-entering) a client system. Able to work out a relationship which has the desired long-run consequences.					
3. **Diagnosis** Examination of the motive of the client. Problem definition and assessment of barriers.					
4. **Data collection** Agreement between client and consultant as to kinds of data to be gathered and methods for doing so.					
5. **Relationship** Working out a constructive mutual acceptance of each other's contribution.					
6. **Resource identification and development** Determining those areas where the consultant and client can be resources to the process.					
7. **Decision making** How decisions will be made and getting them accomplished and acted upon.					
8. **Boundary definition** Agreements as to where the relationship and roles may proceed.					
9. **Ethics and values** Establishing and maintaining a set of values which are kept clear to the client system.					

	Little Ability	Some	Moderate	Considerable	Great Ability

10. **Plans and alternatives**
    Able to effect and successfully work out specific action plans which are tangible and mutually accepted.

11. **Change strategy**
    Consultant's assessing the client's capacity for change and ability to consider and devise strategies which will help the systems to carry out the change plans.

12. **Termination**
    Altering the relationship *as* it progresses and finally terminated without undue strain to the systems.

13. **Evaluation**
    Building in feedback mechanisms which can continuously moniter the change experience.

Select the three concerns that you would like most to work on. Rank these according to your preference:

1. _____

2. _____

3. _____

Consultation-Skills Inventory

This check list is designed to help you think about various aspects of the behaviors involved in consultation. It gives you an opportunity to assess your skills and to set your own goals for growth and development. To use it best:

1. Read through the list of activities and decide which ones you are doing the right amount of, which ones you need to do more of and which ones you need to do less of. Make a check for each item in the appropriate place.

2. Some activities that are important to you may not be listed here. Write these activities on the blank lines.

3. Go back over the whole list and circle the numbers of the three or four activities in which you want most to improve.

General skills	Okay	Need to do more	Need to do less
1. Thinking before I talk	____	____	____
2. Feeling comfortable with my educational background	____	____	____
3. Being brief and concise	____	____	____
4. Understanding my motivation for working in a helping profession	____	____	____
5. Reading group process accurately	____	____	____
6. Separating personal issues and work	____	____	____
7. Listening actively to others	____	____	____
8. Appreciating the impact of my own behavior	____	____	____
9. Being aware of my need to compete with others	____	____	____
10. Dealing with conflict and anger	____	____	____
11. Building an atmosphere of trust and openness	____	____	____
12. Having a clear theory base	____	____	____

Sensing and diagnosing	Okay	Need to do more	Need to do less
13. Helping clients to discover their own problems	_____	_____	_____
14. Asking direct questions	_____	_____	_____
15. Inspiring the client's confidence in my ability to do the job	_____	_____	_____
16. Willing not to be needed by the client	_____	_____	_____
17. Offering to find answers to questions	_____	_____	_____
18. Drawing others out	_____	_____	_____
19. Expecting clients to use my solutions	_____	_____	_____
20. Helping clients generate solutions to their own problems	_____	_____	_____
21. Accepting the client's definition of the problem	_____	_____	_____

Contracting

	Okay	Need to do more	Need to do less
22. Talking about money and fees without embarrassment	_____	_____	_____
23. Promising only what I can deliver	_____	_____	_____
24. Saying "no" without guilt or fear	_____	_____	_____
25. Working under pressure of deadlines and time limits	_____	_____	_____
26. Setting realistic goals for myself and the client	_____	_____	_____
27. Presenting my biases and theoretical foundations	_____	_____	_____
28. Working comfortably with authority figures	_____	_____	_____
29. Letting someone else take the glory	_____	_____	_____
30. Working with people I do not particularly like	_____	_____	_____
31. Giving in to client restrictions and limitations	_____	_____	_____
32. Assessing personal needs that determine acceptance of the contract	_____	_____	_____

Problem solving	Okay	Need to do more	Need to do less
33. Stating problems and objectives clearly	——	——	——
34. Summarizing discussions	——	——	——
35. Selling my own ideas effectively	——	——	——
36. Helping clients maintain a logical sequence of problem solving	——	——	——
37. Challenging ineffective solutions	——	——	——
38. Describing how other clients solved a similar problem	——	——	——
39. Asking for help from others	——	——	——
40. Evaluating possible solutions critically	——	——	——
41. Contributing various techniques for creative problem solving	——	——	——

Implementing			
42. Attending to details	——	——	——
43. Helping clients use their strengths and resources	——	——	——
44. Taking responsibility	——	——	——
45. Changing plans when emergencies come up	——	——	——
46. Building and maintaining morale	——	——	——
47. Requesting feedback about the impact of my presentations	——	——	——
48. Controlling my anxiety while I am performing my task	——	——	——
49. Intervening without threatening my clients	——	——	——
50. Intervening at the appropriate time	——	——	——
51. Admitting errors and mistakes	——	——	——
52. Admitting my own defensiveness	——	——	——

Evaluating	Okay	Need to do more	Need to do less
53. Assessing my own contributions realistically	_____	_____	_____
54. Acknowledging failure	_____	_____	_____
55. Feeling comfortable with clients reviewing my work	_____	_____	_____
56. Dealing with unpredicted changes	_____	_____	_____
57. Devising forms, inventories, etc., to aid evaluation	_____	_____	_____
58. Relying on informal feedback	_____	_____	_____
59. Taking notes, writing up what has been done	_____	_____	_____
60. Letting go when the task is finished	_____	_____	_____
61. Arranging for next steps and follow-up	_____	_____	_____
62. Attributing failure to client's "resistance"	_____	_____	_____

Consulting Roles

Ronald Lippitt and Gordon Lippitt

Consultants must frequently change hats as they shift from one facilitative function to another. Such shifts will be effective and appropriate if the consultant is sufficiently experienced and astute enough to ascertain which role or style is appropriate for which function, situation, and client—and the consultant is proficient in each role's behavioral requirements.

The following discussion presents internal and external consultant roles along a directive to nondirective continuum. By "directive" we refer to situations in which the consultant provides information which clients may or may not choose to use when making organizational decisions.

Advocate

In an advocate role, the consultant endeavors to influence the client, using one of two quite different types of advocacy.

1. **Positional or content advocacy** is a role posture of trying to influence the client to choose particular goals or to accept particular values.
2. **Methodological advocacy** is a role posture of trying to influence the client to become active as a problem solver and to use certain methods of problem solving while being careful not to advocate any particular solution (which would be positional advocacy). In this role, the consultant's behavior takes a "believer" or "valuer" stance about a content or methodological matter.

Technical specialist

The more traditional role of a consultant is that of a specialist who, through special knowledge, skill, and professional experience, is engaged, either through internal employment or under contract, to provide a unique service to an organization. Within this realm of augmenting client expertise, the client is mainly responsible for defining the problem and the objectives of the consultation. Thereafter, the consultant assumes a directive role until the client is comfortable with the particular

approach selected. Later in the relationship, the consultant may act as a catalyst in implementing the recommendations made.

The internal or the external consultant may either be a content specialist on the client's problem or a process specialist on how to cope with a problem. This particular role brings out the consultant's substantive knowledge.

Trainer/educator

Innovative consultation may frequently require the use of periodic or continuous training and education within the client system. In this aspect of the helping relationship, the consultant can play a role in bringing to bear the learning process which best suits the situation and the need. The consultant may be a designer of learning experiences or a direct teacher. In a sense, this role requires the consultant to have the skill of a learning methodologist and manager.

Collaborator in problem solving

The helping role assumed by the consultant in problem solving uses a synergistic approach to complement and collaborate with the client in the perceptual cognitive, and action-taking process needed to solve the problem. The consultant helps maintain objectivity while stimulating conceptual understanding of the problem.

Additionally, the consultant must help isolate and define the "real" dependent and independent variables that influenced the problem's cause, and ultimately its solution. The consultant also assists in weighing alternatives, aids in sorting out salient causal relationships that may affect alternatives, and synthesizes and develops a course of action for an effective resolution. The consultant is involved in the decision-making as a peer member.

Identifier of alternatives

Decisions always involve costs. While the value of a decision depends on the attainment of a given set of objectives, in selecting an appropriate solution to a problem several identifiable alternatives can be proposed, along with their attendant risks. The alternatives, either because of financial or other implications, should be discussed with the client.

In this helping relationship, the consultant must establish relevant criteria for assessing alternatives and develop cause-effect relationships for each alternative along with an appropriate set of strategies. In this particular situational role, however, the consultant does not participate in decision making, but identifies appropriate alternatives facing the problem solver.

Fact finder

Fact finding is an integral part of the consulting process whether it be for developing a data base or for resolving intricate client problems. It is perhaps the most critical area and often the one that receives the least attention in actual problem solving and decision making. It first requires development of criteria and guidelines to be used in the performance of the fact finding process and related analysis. It ends when all available facts have been analyzed and synthesized. The result of this process is giving information to the client for problem solving. Fact finding can be as simple as listening or as complex as a formal survey utilizing a number of techniques. In this role, the consultant functions basically as a researcher.

Process specialist

Here the consultant attempts to help the client become more effective and responsive. The consultant must be concerned specifically with the work process as a way of achieving client adaptability. As a process specialist, the consultant must sharpen all of his or her multiple role skills to help the client. The consultant works on developing joint client-consultant diagnostic skills for addressing specific and relevant problems to focus on how things are done rather than what tasks are performed. The consultant helps the client integrate interpersonal and group skills and events with task-oriented activities and to observe the best match of relationships. In this role, the consultant functions as a giver of feedback.

Reflector

When operating as a reflector, the consultant stimulates the client to make decisions by asking reflective questions which may help to clarify, or change a given situation. In this role the consultant may be an arbitrator, an integrator, or an empathetic respondent who experiences along with the client those blocks which provided the structure and provoked the situation initially. The consultant acts as philosopher.

Third-Party Consultation

John J. Sherwood

The presence of a third-party consultant sets the stage or produces the following:

1. Some optimism among the parties that relief or resolution is forthcoming.

2. More parity to each party's position, plus neutrality—i.e., when the consultant makes a low investment in a winner.

3. Support within which to take risks, plus credibility—yet low power over the parties by the third party.

4. A challenge to complacency or avoidance.

The third party brings the following:

1. Concepts to clarify conflict—e.g., define areas of contention (jurisdictional, role definitional, interpersonal style, etc.); what are objectives of each party; notions such as expanding space, limiting contact; noting that strategies such as win/lose often lead to lose/lose outcomes; conflict often appears at the lowest power positions within an organization (e.g., between workers rather than between boss and subordinate or between boss and boss); conflict can be moved so it can be addressed where it originated; conflicts are probably best worked out at their origin.

2. The third party is a manager—providing procedures to guide parties with high control over the structure of their meeting.

3. Feedback and clarifying skills. The third party also models listening, feedback, confronting differences, and recognizing agreements.

4. A moderate knowledge of the parties and their differences (it is important that both parties "know" that the consultant views each as a person of worth).

The Role of the Consultant

Examine each statement and using the key provided below, decide on the extent to which *you* agree or disagree with the statement. Put the appropriate symbol in the space provided before the statement. If you are a member of a consultant team, after each member has rated each statement, take about 30 minutes to share and discuss the similarities and differences.

    SA = Strongly Agree
     A = Agree
     U = Undecided
     D = Disagree
    SD = Strongly Disagree

1. _____ If a consultant has been asked to conduct an off-site team-building session and learns before the event that the team leader has been fired, he/she should arrange for the leader to remain on the job until the meeting is completed.

2. _____ Work with the forces in the organization that support change and improvement, rather than work against those who are defensive and resistant.

3. _____ An internal OD consultant's influence is based upon her or his authority and power as much as it is on expertise and ability to help.

4. _____ An OD consultant can make a more significant impact by linking together people who are working to improve the organization so that their abilities reinforce and complement one another.

5. _____ Most people doing team building these days do an effective job of helping their client groups feel responsible for their own improvement.

6. _____ Ultimately, the question for the internal person will be: "Given my location in the hierarchy and prevailing organizational climate, what is it possible for us to accomplish here?"

7. _____ The OD consultant with a long-term contract has an obligation to develop an internal capacity in the client organization to carry out the planned change effort and to ultimately withdraw as the primary change-agent/consultant.

8. _____ In the team setting the consultant should remain objective and not initiate confrontations.

9. _____ The consultant must help the client delineate when he or she needs to be dependent and when he or she does not.

10. _____ Make the boss your client. If you make "the group" your client, you will be seen as naive because everyone knows that the boss has to take the risks.

11. _____ If you sense that the boss is nervous about the team at the beginning of your project, meet with him/her alone at the beginning.

12. _____ It is fairly common for OD consultants to accept statements from clients that they don't want to work together, can't work together, and have no reason to work together.

13. _____ The role of the OD consultant is to prepare managers to develop the organization and plan change—important work for which they have not been trained previously.

Observations of Consultant's Behavior: Potential Diary Questions

Entry phase

1. Reactions to consultant's introduction of self.

2. Was rapport established? Note specific behaviors.

3. If you were the client would you be comfortable with the consultant in this early phase of their relationship? What did consultant contribute to the client's feelings of comfort *and* discomfort?

4. Are the parameters of the consultation established (objectives, roles, timing, etc.)? What remains to be done?

5. Does the consultant seem aware of the client's feelings?

Work phase

6. Reactions to consultant as meeting progresses (watch body language and facial expressions for insights into interest, nervousness, comfort level, hostility).

7. Is the consultant listening? Note instances of not listening.

8. Is the consultant interested in the client? How do you know?

9. If you were the client would you be comfortable with the consultant at this time?

Closure Phase

10. Reactions to the way consultant handles the end of meeting.

11. Was a clear and useful summary provided?

12. Are the next steps clear? (What may be points of unclarity or uncertainty?)

13. Based on your observations of this meeting alone, would you ask the consultant back? Why? Why not?

14. In what ways was the meeting *useful* to the client? In what ways was the meeting a *problem* for the client?

Issues to Consider When Consulting

PAUL BUCHANAN

The following issues must be considered when a consultant attempts to help an organization develop its effectiveness:

1. Who is the "client"? That is, one must distinguish "target" and "beneficiary" populations and identify any existing "leverage" groups.

2. In what areas will the different populations accept, push for, or resist change?

3. Clarify or develop the client's motivation to change.

4. Assess the change-agent's potential helpfulness regarding: relevance of resources, interests, and competence to the client's need; job security in relation to the client system;

- relevance of resources, interests, and competence to the client's need;
- job security in relation to the client system;
- relations among members of the change-agent team;
- compatibility of different objectives (for example, to help the client, to conduct research, to get promoted within the company);
- time available.

5. Establish effective relations between the change-agent and the client system including the following:

- the role of each in planning and conducting the program;
- expectations regarding the amount and kind of effort required of each in the change program;
- restrictions (if any) upon the kinds of changes allowed;
- expectations regarding the role(s) or kind(s) of help the change-agent is to provide.

6. Clarify or diagnose the client system's problems:

- determine how information is to be obtained and from whom;

- identify use of data in diagnosis;
- develop diagnostic skills of members of the system;
- determine the boundaries of the client system.

7. Establish instrumental objectives for change (How should we operate?).

8. Formulate plans for change:

- create links to other persons, issues, and parts within the client system;
- create links to other persons, parts, and issues in the external system;
- develop schedule and establish time expectations;
- develop procedures and structures for carrying out plans;
- provide anticipatory testing of plans;
- develop competence of those taking actions;
- develop motivation for carrying out plans.

9. Carry out plans for change:

- maintain support and understanding from the larger system;
- obtain feedback on consequences of early action steps;
- coordinate efforts of different people and groups involved.

10. Generalize and stabilize changes:

- assess the effects of the change upon the total system;
- look for "regression";
- facilitate spread to other parts of target system and to adjacent interdependent systems.

11. Institutionalize planned development or self-renewal:

- develop problem-sensing and problem-solving skills and mechanisms in all components of the system;
- develop a reward system which facilitates innovation;
- establish a change-agent role in the system.

A Four-phase Developmental Model of the Consultative Relationship*

PHASE	STYLE OF REQUEST	CONSULTANT ROLE FUNCTIONS	CLIENT ROLE FUNCTIONS
I.	INITIAL MAGICAL THINKING-TESTING "You know what we need; do it for us." "Take care of us."	*Actively model* (1) assessing needs, (2) setting objectives, (3) analyzing problems, (4) developing change strategies and action plans, (5) implementing planned change interventions, (6) coordinating and (7) monitoring intervention activities. *Provide* theoretical/explanatory concepts. Close, on-going *contact* is essential.	*Actively* (1) observe consultant's execution of these seven consultant role functions, (2) provide/disclose information/opinions requested by consultant, (3) follow instructions/directions given by consultant and (4) acquire mastery of explanatory concepts. (If in discharging these role functions the clients' strongly held values or beliefs are violated, consider terminating the contract.)
II.	DEPENDENCY-ACCEPTANCE "Tell us what to do and we'll do it." "You're the expert, give us the formula."	*Collaboratively* (1) implement and (2) monitor intervention activities. *Actively* (1) *model* (a) analyzing implementation problems, (b) modifying change strategies and action plans, (c) coordinating and (d) evaluating intervention effects; and (2) provide (a) theoretical concepts, (b) skill training experiences and (c) coaching for feedback to clients on the quality and effectiveness of their interventions. Close, on-going *contact* desirable, not vital.	*Collaboratively* (1) implement and (2) monitor intervention activities. *Actively* (a) observe consultant's execution of these role functions, (2) provide all requested information/opinions, (3) follow all agreed-with directions from consultant, (4) seek coaching/feedback from consultant and peers on own intervention activities, (5) acquire conceptual mastery and (6) skills in facilitating planned change.
III.	EMERGENCE OF COMPETENCE "Let us do it; but don't go too far away in case we need support." "How are we doing?" "Help us improve on our performance."	*Passive* in implementing interventions. *Collaboratively* (1) monitoring implementation problems, (2) analyzing implementation problems, (3) modifying change strategies, (4) evaluating intervention effects and (5) provide coaching and feedback. *Actively* coordinate implementation of intervention plans. Regularly scheduled *follow-up* is vital.	*Actively* (1) implementing intervention activities, (2) seeking feedback and coaching, (3) acquiring conceptual mastery, (4) acquiring skills, (5) experimenting with applying concepts and skills, (6) providing feedback and (7) observing consultant executive role functions. *Collaboratively* (1) monitor implementation, (2) analyze problems, (3) modify strategies and plans and (4) evaluate effects.
IV.	EMERGENCE OF SELF-SUFFICIENCY "We want to do it ourselves." [OR: INITIAL COUNTER-DEPENDENCY] "Prove that we need your help." "We've tried everything to change this situation; nothing works; you can't help."	*Collaboratively* (1) coordinate intervention plans and (2) conduct "case consultations" around problems encountered by clients during their experiences with the planned change process. Scheduled *follow-up* is highly desirable. *Collaboratively* conduct one or more "what went wrong?" problem clinics. Employ the "FLEXIBLE IS FUNCTIONAL" diagnostic model. If this seems to reduce or neutralize the counter-dependent attitudes and behavior of the clients, *shift to PHASE I or II*. If ineffective, *terminate the contract.*	*Collaboratively* (1) coordinate and (2) participate in "case consultations." *Actively* perform all other planned change role functions, keeping detailed notes on problems encountered (for "case consultations").

*Based on the article by Steve Ruma in *Social Change*, 4(4), 1974. © 1974. NTL Institute. Adapted by Arthur M. Freedman.

Pre-entry Issues in Consultation*

Cary Cherniss

Long before the first approach to a potential client system, a consultant confronts several fundamental issues contained in the consultation process. The ways in which the consultant resolves these issues will substantially influence the consultant's thinking and action throughout the consultation. The consultant's position on these issues also will determine how he or she will be regarded by clients. These "pre-entry" issues are important because, if the consultant does not think them through carefully (which often happens), the result frequently is unnecessary confusion and ambiguity about the consultant's role and mission. And, as research has suggested, such ambiguity is often associated with less effective consultation (Mann, 1973). Finally, an adequate consideration of these pre-entry issues helps the consultant deal with subsequent issues and problems.

As will be noted below, consultation can and is defined differently, depending on how the consultant answers the pre-entry questions. Generally, consultation may be defined as a process in which one or more individuals, possessing certain knowledge and skills, help other individuals and groups within a particular social system work on one or more work-related problems. This definition of consultation includes the work of Caplan (1970), Argyris (1970) and Sarason, Levine, Goldenberg, Cherlin and Bennett (1966).

The pre-entry issues of consultation include

"Should one do consultation in this situation?"

"Whose interests will the consultant serve?"

"What will be the primary focus of consultation?"

Unfortunately, few consultants have considered these fundamental questions in any systematic way. Much has been written about entry, but the equally important issues that temporarily and conceptually precede entry have been relatively neglected.

Should one provide consultation in this situation?

There are always alternatives to consultation. The most experienced, effective consultants consider the alternatives carefully each time they have an opportunity to provide consultation. They do not compulsively seize at any invitation they receive. Rather, they evaluate the situation according to a previously conceived set of criteria. Less effective consultants, on the other hand, do not seem to possess a set of criteria for deciding this question; in fact, in many instances, they do not even seem to see this question as worthy of consideration.

For instance, a short time ago, I participated in a meeting of a school consultation project. One of the consultants had had an opportunity to meet regularly with an administrator in a school system where mental health consultation was being delivered. Most members of the project seemed to feel that this was certainly a fortunate opportunity. However, the meetings with the consultee were considered by the consultant who attended them to be unproductive and he thus raised the question: Why should we provide consultation to this person?

The initial response to the question was silence. The silence finally was broken by one individual's somewhat hesitant and confused explanation that consultation should be provided to the administrator because he had made himself available and because he had "high status in the system."

Agreeing to consult with someone in a system simply because he has "high status" does not seem to provide a clear, strong rationale for the consultation. This group of experienced, professional mental health consultants obviously had not given much thought to an important pre-entry question.

The question, "to consult or not to consult," is important and useful because it forces the consultant to consider the "universe of alternatives." As Sarason (1971) has observed, carefully considering the possible alternatives to any course of action prevents one from acting in stereotyped, ineffective ways. It helps liberate one from the shackles of tradition and it forces one to confront fundamental issues. Thus, by self-consciously asking whether or not to consult in a particular situation, the consultant will more likely become aware of

*From *American Journal of Community Psychology*, 1976, 4(1), 13-24.

alternatives to consultation. Then, after deciding to consult, it will be in the context of a careful examination of alternative ways of proceeding; such a stance ultimately will be liberating for both the consultant and the client.

The question of whether or not one should accept an invitation to consult is important not only because it seems to provide the basis for more effective consultation, but also because of economic considerations. As Sarason (1969) pointed out in another context, we do not now have nor will we probably ever have enough consultants to help all of the social systems that need help. Thus, a consultant who agrees to work within a system is tying up a substantial amount of professional time and energy. Agreeing to consult to one system limits a consultant's ability to consult to other systems. Of course, consultants can and do work in more than one system. Their capacity to give help, however, ultimately is limited, and they will have little time for future requests or opportunities to consult. Thus, for economic reasons, a socially responsible consultant will weigh the question of whether to consult in a particular situation carefully before making a major commitment of consultative time and energy.

The decision to consult suggests two types of alternatives. First, one may wish to intervene in a particular situation, but not through the method of consultation. As Caplan (1970) and others have suggested, it is only one of many types of "social interventions" that can be employed (Hornstein, Bunker, Burke, Gindes & Lewicki, 1971). Investigative reporting (e.g., Chu, 1973), the creation of alternative settings (Sarason, 1972), political action (Alinsky, 1971), or direct service delivery are other ways of confronting problems that exist in social systems. Thus, even when it is appropriate to intervene in a particular situation, consultation may not be the "method of choice."[1]

The question of whether or not one should consult also suggests that one may not wish to intervene at all in a particular situation. Some social systems and situations will not be amenable to any constructive intervention at a particular time. Thus, one may decline to consult in a particular situation in favor of more promising ones.

Bases for answering the question

Value Congruence. Whether or not the consultant consciously thinks through this basic question, it is answered in some way; the answer will be influenced by a number of factors. One basis for answering the question is value congruence. For instance, Levine (1969) writes:

The goals or the values of the helping agent or the helping

[1]In some cases, empirical research can help a consultant answer this and other pre-entry questions. For instance, future research could suggest the system or target characteristic that dictates consultation rather than another type of intervention.

service must be consistent with the goals or the values of the setting in which the problem is manifested. This postulate assumes that settings have important major purposes and that the achievement of these purposes is vital to the continuance of the setting. It further assumes that the setting will act to expel or otherwise make ineffective those helping agents who promote goals or values at variance with the major goals and values of the setting. (pp. 218-219)

During recent years, I have seen numerous examples in consultation practice that confirm Levine's premise. On more than one occasion I have witnessed individuals who were committed to a "radical-humanistic" conception of education assume the role of consultation in the public school system. In virtually every case I know of, the consultation failed, either with a "bang" (the consultants eventually were asked to leave, or with a "whimper" (the consultants—discouraged, hurt, and frustrated—eventually left without any sense of accomplishment). In such instances, it probably would have been better if the consultants had asked themselves if they should consult in these situations and had considered the congruence between their own values and those of the potential client system.

In many instances, consultants do answer the question negatively because of ethical or value considerations. For instance, despite Bard's eloquent pleas that mental health workers consult with police departments (Bard, 1971), I know of many consultants who will not do so because the police represent values and purposes they regard as socially destructive. Thus, value congruence should be and often is an important consideration in deciding whether consultation should be provided in any given situation.

Resources. A second basis for determining whether one should consult in a situation is the relationship between the consultant's resources of time and expertise and the resources required to consult effectively in the situation. A consultant is being asked to devote a certain amount of time and to call upon certain types of knowledge and skills. Instances will arise when a consultant should decline to consult, lacking the time or technical resources necessary to help the people involved.

Unfortunately, consultants do not always confront the problem of resources when deciding whether they should consult. A request that one provide consultation to an individual or group often flatters a consultant and generates a powerful sense of mission to alleviate suffering or to right some wrong. Feeling flattered and wanting to save people, however, may lead a consultant to ignore the problem of resources. Such a situation may result in a failure to assess accurately the relationship between the resources required and the resources available. One way to prevent these problems is for would-be consultants always to be aware of and make known to the client their own particular knowledge, skills, and time constraints.

Client Characteristics. A third basis for deciding

whether to consult in a particular situation is the characteristics of the client. Previous experience and writing on the consultation process suggest a number of characteristics that could be relevant. For instance, Caplan (1970) has observed that best results in mental health consultation seem to occur with clients who are most upset by or concerned about their problems. Thus, the client's motivation to change could be an important consideration in deciding whether to consult in a particular situation.

Another writer on the consultation process, Chris Argyris (1970), will only consult to client systems that are "open to and capable of learning" and that provide the consultant access to "the power points in the client system that are the keys to the problem being studied." Argyris also will avoid situations in which proposals for change will be imposed on any part of the organization (Argyris, 1970, pp. 25-26). Not everyone will agree with Argyris's criteria, and exactly how one would assess a potential client system's "openness to learning" is not clear. Nevertheless, Argyris's criteria do suggest that one basis for deciding whether to consult is the presence or absence of certain characteristics in the client system. Undoubtedly, many experienced consultants do consider characteristics in the client system when deciding whether to consult. Many others, however, do not seem to consider systematically client characteristics as a basis for answering the question. As a result, they often find themselves enmeshed in consultations of limited value.

The influence of the social milieu. Consultants, like the rest of humanity, do not operate in a social vacuum. First, consultants always work in a particular institutional context, and the norms, traditions, policies, and economics of the consultant's institution will influence when and where consultants intervene. For instance, university-based consultants are part of an institution that traditionally values teaching and research (Cherniss, 1972; Nisbet, 1971). These consultants will most likely consult in situations in which one has an opportunity to pursue research of some sort and to teach students. For the individual working in a profit-making consulting firm, economic factors will play a large role in determining whether consultation is provided in a particular situation. Public-sector consultants are also sensitive to financial considerations, since consultation frequently is a more marginal activity in their settings (e.g., community mental health centers) and must often "pay its own way" (Reiff, 1966; Cherniss, in press).

In addition to their institutional context, consultants are influenced by the ideas and social forces that shape the "spirit of the times." The prevailing *zeitgeist* makes certain issues, problems, and even professional theories and methods seem more "important" and "timely" (Levine & Levine, 1970). Historical forces influence the consultant directly as an individual and they also influence the institutional context in which the consultant works. For instance, when the Soviet Union launched its Sputnik in 1958, it damaged American pride and aroused concern with the quality of public education (Sarason, 1974). During the next decade, growing numbers of professionals from education, mental health, and organizational science worked in public school settings. In the later part of the 1960s, however, spurred in part by the Nixon administration's emphasis on "law and order" and the growing unrest among prison inmates, correctional settings were increasingly identified as targets for consultation (e.g., Reppucci, Sarata, Saunders, McArthur & Michlin, 1973, Sarason, 1974; Katkin & Sibley, 1973; Levine, Geisomino, Joss & Ayer, 1973). Most recently, there has been growing pressure in a number of states to substantially reduce state mental hospital populations. To accommodate the growing numbers of discharged mental patients, various types of community-living facilities have been created, and many community mental health professionals have provided consultation to these settings. Thus, the "spirit of the times" as well as the specific institutional context in which one works will influence a consultant's decisions about the desirability of consulting in any given situation.

Effective consultants recognize that numerous alternatives exist and that consultation in a particular situation is but one of them. Also, they realize that they have only limited time and resources and that the decision to provide consultation should be weighed carefully. In deciding whether to consult, one inevitably confronts such issues as one's own values and their congruence with those of the client, the relationship between the consultant's present resources and those required to consult effectively, certain client characteristics, and the consultant's own social milieu.

Whose interests will the consultant serve?

All social settings are characterized by conflict and competition between diverse interest groups. These groups are aware of their differences and, when a consultant enters a setting, they are anxious to see whose interests the consultant will represent. If consultants do not think through this issue before entering a setting, their behavior will appear ambiguous and confusing to clients, trust between consultant and clients will develop slowly at best, and consultation will be less effective.

The constituency issue is also important because its resolution will influence how consultants define their role, what immediate and long-term goals they will pursue, and what strategies and techniques they will use. Some potential implications of the question are discussed in the following example suggested by Seymour Sarason.

Suppose one has agreed to consult in an elementary school classroom where many problems have occurred. Suppose further that the consultant is one who often helps clients learn and use behavioral techniques to better manage problems in their own work settings. Preliminary observation in the classroom suggests to the consultant that a modification of certain reinforcement contingencies will improve the situation. But whom will the consultant train in the use of the technique? This may seem to be an odd question because most consultants would teach the techniques to the teacher without even thinking that there might be an alternative.

But recall the proposition that all social settings are characterized by conflict and competition between diverse interest groups. Waller (1967) argued that in the classroom, the teacher and the students represent different and usually antagonistic interests. They have different "agendas" and "priorities." Thus, in choosing to train the teacher in the use of behavioral technology, our hypothetical consultant has made an important decision (a decision that probably was made before entry and with little awareness). The consultant could have chosen at least two other approaches in the situation: offering training and consultation just to the students or to both the students and the teacher. A recognition that competing interests were involved, and a careful consideration of the question, "Whose interests will I serve?" could lead the consultant to very different decisions about role, strategy, and goals, and probably would facilitate development of the consultant-client relationship.

Unfortunately, consultants often ignore the constituency issue by refusing to accept the existence of competing interests in social settings. Many consultants attempt to sidestep the issue by believing that ultimately everyone is interested in the same goals. In these cases consultants attempt to avoid taking a stand by asserting that they are "everybody's" agent or even that their constituency is "society." Such platitudes may help consultants to dismiss a sensitive and complex issue and "in the long run" there may even be some truth to the claims. Consultants working in the world of action, however, never deal with the "long run"; they face various interest groups that are primarily concerned with very different goals. Unless consultants clarify their own stance before the entry phase begins and communicate that stance to the clients, consultation may falter from ambiguity and mistrust.

What will be the primary focus of the consultation?

Before approaching a potential consultation, the consultant usually has selected a primary focus. The focus may not be articulated to others, and the consultant may not even be aware of having selected a guide for future thinking and actions. Choosing the primary focus, however, is another important pre-entry issue which must be considered.

Four areas of focus in consultation

The primary focus in most consultation work tends to be in one of four areas: organizational structure and process; technology; the mental health of individuals; and the group or organizational environment. To clarify how each of these can serve as a primary focus of consultation, let us examine them in the context of one possible client setting, a public elementary school.

Some consultants to a school setting will tend to focus on organizational structure and process (e.g., Argyris, 1970). They will be concerned with how well the internal social organization of the school functions. They will assess communication patterns, decision making, interpersonal relations, morale, and performance. Their basic mission is to identify obstacles to adaptive organizational functioning and recommend modifications intended to rectify the problems. Consultants who take this focus may assume that an improvement in the school's organizational functioning will benefit the mental health of individuals, the educational process, and the welfare of the entire community. They focus primarily on the organization and its properties, however, and a better internal climate and effective problem solving are their primary goals.

Other consultants in this situation will focus on the technology. In a public school, this would be the educational process as it occurs within the classroom. A specific example would be a consultant who helps teachers transform their classes into "open classrooms." Such a consultant focuses on how the teacher thinks about, organizes, and conducts the educational process. The primary goals are to make the teacher a better teacher and the classroom a richer learning environment. By "technology" I mean the skills, techniques, and processes required to perform a particular task. In the case of educational, correctional, and mental health settings, however, "technology" as I am using it here also includes knowledge, values, and even personal feelings that are critical ingredients in performance of the teaching or helping process.

The mental health of individuals is yet another possible primary focus for consultation. When mental health is the focus, the consultant ultimately is concerned with the cognitive and effective functioning of particular individuals. Although the consultant may never see these individuals, the goal of the intervention is to bring about change that will facilitate either treatment or prevention of individual emotional problems. In the school setting, a mental health consultant spends much time helping the staff work more effectively with students who manifest some type of behavioral problem (cf. Caplan, 1970; Sarason et al., 1966). When not concerned with a particular student, a mental health consultant will tend to engage in activities closely related to student mental health (e.g., helping school staff set up an early identification program for "high risk" students).

Still other consultants tend to focus on the group or

organizational environment. In the school setting, such a consultant may be concerned with school-community relations and an attempt to help the school staff develop more effective community programs. The ultimate goal is harmonious, mutually satisfying, and beneficial relations between the school and its surrounding community. Staff morale, the quality of the teaching process and student mental health are not of primary concern to this consultant. Like the other consultants, however, this one may assume that the primary focus, better school-community relations, will improve functioning in other areas as well.

It can be argued that these areas of primary focus in practice are mutually exclusive. A "mental health" consultant may—some would say should—also become highly involved in organizational, technological, and community issues. In reality, one's primary focus is constantly shifting, and it should shift as the situation dictates to maximize the consultant's effectiveness. Some may also argue (e.g., Sarason et al., 1966) that initially a consultant should avoid assuming a primary focus; the focus should be formulated in collaboration with the clients and based on a careful assessment of current needs and problems.

Consultants often work on more than one type of concern and, during the course of a consultation, the focus may shift. An individual consultant, however, usually does assume some kind of primary focus and in some way communicates this focus to the clients.

Identifying a primary focus does not "hem in" consultants or make their roles too inflexible. Each offers a wide latitude of possible activities in which the consultants may engage. For instance, a mental health consultant may work with individuals or with groups, with line staff or with administrators, on specific cases, on the clients' own skills, or on programs. In all these instances, however, the consultant may retain a primary focus on the mental health of individuals.

Many consultants, in an effort to "keep their options open," attempt to avoid answering the question, "What will be the primary focus of the consultation?" In every case I know of, such a maneuver merely impeded the consultation. As with the other pre-entry questions, a consultant's failure to consider this one confuses the client about the nature of the consultant's role and thus interferes with consultation effectiveness. Flexibility in role is one of the unique advantages available to a consultant; however, role flexibility is different from the ambiguity, confusion, and manipulativeness that arise when a consultant attempts to avoid an identification with a primary focus.

Bases for answering the question

Many factors will influence a consultant's choice of primary focus. For instance, a consultant's values and conception of society may lead to a favoring of one primary focus over another. Similarly, the policies and mission of a consultant's own institution may strongly influence the choice of focus. A consultant working out of a mental health agency will not only be expected to focus on mental health issues by colleagues and superiors, but also by clients (Cherniss, in press). Naturally, a consultant's training and experiences also will influence which primary focus is chosen. A school consultant who has extensively studied educational theory and practice will tend to focus on the technology, while a school consultant who has studied organizational and administrative theory will tend to focus on organizational functioning. Personal style and aptitude may be yet another factor influencing choice of focus.

The choice of primary focus has a number of implications for the consultation process. First, a consultant's primary focus may influence when and where the consultation occurs. It may also influence the entry process, the initial activities in which the consultant engages, and the initial "diagnostic questions" that are emphasized. In short, the decision concerning primary focus, made before contact with the client, influences a number of subsequent decisions and actions.

Conclusion

Certain basic questions of consultation should be confronted in some way by the consultant before "entry" and often before any contact is made with the client system. Observation of consultants at work suggests that these pre-entry questions are rarely articulated explicitly, and failure to do so seems to impede consultant effectiveness. Thinking through these questions helps a consultant make more rational, coherent choices about many of the issues that arise during the consultation and minimizes much of the ambiguity, conflict, and confusion that interfere with effective intervention.

Some of these questions can only be answered in the process of entry. For instance, deciding whether one should provide consultation in a particular situation requires some information. Much of this information can only be gathered during the entry process. Also, the nature of the contract negotiated between consultant and client during entry may resolve (or exacerbate) some of the pre-entry issues that have been discussed.

While many of these issues cannot be resolved before entry, they should be and can be considered before entry begins. A consultant often must initiate entry to decide whether consultation would be appropriate; but the idea that "whether or not to consult" is an issue, and the criteria to be used in evaluating it, should be formulated before entry begins.

In conclusion, I believe there is a pressing need for models or theories of consultation that include clear answers to the pre-entry questions. In this sense I endorse Lewin's now-famous statement that there is nothing so practical as a good theory. I also believe that while formal models are necessary, however, they are not sufficient prerequisites for effective consultation. Effective consultants are guided by theory, but they also are guided by a store of knowledge concerning actual consultation experiences. They have observed, both directly and indirectly, choices and actions made by consultants and the events that followed. Effective consultants not only have studied the pre-entry issues in consultation, they also have devoted time to the study of the natural history of consultation practice.

References

Alinsky, S. D. *Rules for radicals*. New York: Vintage, 1971.

Argyris. C. *Intervention theory and method*. Reading, Mass.: Addison-Wesley, 1970.

Bard, M. The role of law enforcement in the helping system. *Community Mental Health Journal*, 1971, *7*, 151-160.

Caplan, G. *The theory and practice of mental health consultation*. New York: Basic Books, 1970.

Cherniss, C. *New settings in the University: Their creation, problems, and early development*. Unpublished doctoral dissertation, Yale University, 1972.

Cherniss, C. Creating new consultation programs in community mental health centers: Analysis of a case study. *Community Mental Health Journal*, in press.

Chu, F. *Nader's raiders look at community mental health centers*. Speech delivered before National Council of Community Mental Health Centers, February 26, 1973.

Hornstein, A. A., Bunker, B. B., Burke, W. W., Gindes, M. & Lewicki, R. J. *Social intervention: A behavioral science approach*. New York: Free Press, 1971.

Katkin, E. S., & Sibley, R. F. Psychological consultation at Attica State Prison: Post-hoc reflections on some precursors to a disaster. In I. I. Goldenberg (Ed.), *The helping professions in the world of action*. Boston: D.C. Heath & Co., 1973, 165-194.

Levine, M. Postulates of community psychology practice. In F. Kaplan & S. B. Sarason (Eds.), *The Yale Psycho-Educational Clinic: Papers and research studies*. Boston: Massachusetts Dept. of Mental Health (Community Mental Health Monograph), 1969.

Levine, M., Gelsomino, J., Joss, R. H., & Ayer, W. The "consumer's" perspective of rehabilitative services in a county penitentiary. *International Journal of Mental Health*, 1973, *2(2)*, 94-110.

Levine, M., & Levine. A. *A social history of helping services*. New York: Appleton-Century-Crofts, 1970.

Mann, P. Student consultants: Evaluations by consultees. *American Journal of Community Psychology*, 1973, *1*, 182-193.

Nisbet, R. A. *The degradation of the academic dogma*. New York: Oxford University Press. 1971.

Reiff, R. Mental health manpower and institutional change. *American Psychologist*, 1966, *21*, 540-548.

Reppucci, N. D., Sarata, B. P. V., Saunders, J. T., McArthur, A. V., & Michlin, L. M. We bombed in Mountville: Lessons learned in consultation to a correctional facility for adolescent offenders. In I. I. Goldenberg (Ed.), *The helping professions in the world of action*. Boston: D. C. Heath & Co., 1973, 145-164.

Sarason, S. B. The creation of settings: A preliminary statement. In F. Kaplan & S. B. Sarason (Eds.), *The Yale Psycho-Educational Clinic: Papers and research studies*. Boston: Massachusetts State Dept. of Mental Health (Monograph Series), 1969, 197-207.

Sarason, S. B. *The culture of the school and the problem of change*. Boston: Allyn & Bacon. 1971.

Sarason, S. B. *The creation of settings and the future societies*. San Francisco: Jossey-Bass, 1972.

Sarason, S. B. *The psychological sense of community: Prospects for a community psychology*. San Francisco: Jossey-Bass, 1974.

Sarason, S. B., Levine, M., Goldenberg, I. I., Cherlin, D. L., & Bennett, E. M. *Psychology in community settings: Clinical, vocational, educational, social aspects*. New York: Wiley, 1966.

Waller, W. *The sociology of teaching*. New York: Wiley, 1967.

The Entry Problem in Consultation*

JOHN C. GLIDEWELL

The aim of this paper is to contribute to the definition of a complex problem—the problem faced by a consultant and a client when they first try to enter into a working relationship. It would be presumptuous to propose a solution to such a knotty problem. It seems more appropriate and realistic to limit this paper to defining the problem.

This article is based upon the assumption that the entry of the consultant is a special case of a more general problem: the attachment of a new person to an existing social system. Examples might include the introduction into a family of a tutor for a child temporarily unable to attend school, the attachment of a social-work consultant to a teaching staff, or the introduction of a human-relations consultant to a corporation board. In each case the members of a functioning social system find that some operations are being initiated and performed by a new person. The new person, being a consultant, is presumably authoritative, and also, being new, he or she is relatively unpredictable. Some relationship to this new person must be developed so that the consultant's performance, and the responses of others to it, can be better predicted. Predictability will make performance more amenable to control in the interests of the goals of the system—both substantive achievement goals and affiliative human-relations goals.

Limitations on the problem

For the purposes at hand, "attachment to a social system" will refer to the process of development of relationships with a person who is to be only temporarily a member of the system. It will not refer to the process of development of relationships with a person who is to be a permanent member of the system.[1] The consultant role is often established these days as a permanent one, but this permanence involves either the development of a new role and, therefore, a basic structural change, or it involves the socialization of a new person into an existing role. Both are more fundamental processes than can be

explored here.

Accordingly, this paper is limited to the exploration of the process of initiating a relationship between a client system and a temporary consultant. The consultation functions are to be performed temporarily, either because the need is temporary or because the functions can be taken over—after a time—by existing roles.

Consultant vs. consultant-trainer

One must differentiate those functions that terminate at the expiration of a short-term need from those that are taken over and continued by existing roles. The first requires the application of objects, skills, ideas, or feelings that the client need never possess or control—like prescribing medication, or greasing an auto. The second requires that the client acquire possession and control of the objects, skills, ideas, or feelings, and it, therefore, implies learning—like the improvement of a golf swing, or the recognition of the proper consistency of a pancake batter. The first relationship involves a consultant role; the second, a consultant-trainer role. This article discusses both roles. The distinction should be kept in mind, however, because the role of the consultant provokes less concern about demands for change in the system than does the consultant-trainer role.

Organizational attachment and predictability

A basic criterion of attachment to a social system is predictability. This is a special case of the general proposition that a basic criterion of the existence and nature of relationships is predictability. The statement of lawful

---

[1]The term "attachment to a social system" was borrowed from Jules Henry (1959), who uses it to refer to the state of being an integral part of a social system. It is in no way limited to temporary membership. For present purposes, however, "attachment" seems to imply a temporary arrangement as intended here. Perhaps the appropriate analogy is the military arrangements by which a person who is "attached" to an organization is only temporarily associated with it and entitled to only limited support from the organization.

*Reprinted from *The Journal of Social Issues, 25*(2), 51-59. © 1969 Society for the Psychological Study of Social Issues, a division of the American Psychological Association. Used by permission.

relationships takes the form of predicting some aspect of one object or force from a knowledge of other objects or forces.

Any application of this proposition to social relations must take account of the notion that social systems develop ultimate values and immediate goals. For the members of the system, the significant predictability for social roles is the forecast of performance in relation to ultimate values and immediate goals. The kinds of relationships to be developed in the process of attachment to a social system are those that ensure not that one knows just what a member will do in a given situation but that whatever the member does will contribute to ultimate values and immediate goals. If the people in the system value creativity and invention, it may be important that the exact nature of the performance be unpredictable—so long as its goal orientation is assured. To illustrate, you do not need to predict just what sort of medicine a doctor will give you when you are sick. It is quite important, however, to ensure that the physician contributes to the ultimate value of survival—i.e., that she or he doesn't kill you—and to the immediate goal of relief from distress and disability.

A redefinition of the problem

From the foregoing conceptions, limitations, and distinctions, the entry problem can be redefined as that of initiating the development of relationships to provide a basis for predicting the contribution to ultimate values and immediate goals of a set of functions having certain characteristics, namely the following:

—They are now needed by the system, although probably to a different degree by different members.

—They either are needed only temporarily or can be taken over by existing roles.

—They are not now available in the system.

—They can be performed expertly by the prospective consultant.

The entry problem becomes more or less difficult, depending upon the "goodness of fit" between the consultant and the client system with respect to stabilities and change tendencies in terms of perception of need, assignment of values, role expectation, resource and reward allocation, and feelings about the control of dependency. Goodness of fit is intended to imply both congruence (of values) and complementarity (of roles). The significant dimensions to be fitted can be outlined as follows:

1. Perception of need, in terms of the

    a. extent of consensus in the total system that an immediate need exists, and
    b. importance of the need as measured against the ultimate values of the total system.

2. Perception of appropriateness of role allocation by those empowered to allocate roles, in terms of the criteria that

    a. the needed resources are not available through appropriate persons within the system, and
    b. the needed resources are available through the prospective consultant.

3. Perception of the appropriateness of resource distribution of those empowered to distribute resources, in terms of the criteria that

    a. the consultant will be available to the different members on an equitable basis, and
    b. any new objects, ideas, skills, or feelings developed by the consultation will be equitably distributed.

4. Perception of the appropriateness of reward distribution by those empowered to distribute rewards, in terms of the criteria that

    a. the consultant's fee is appropriate to the need (relative to other needs), and of the quality and quantity of service proposed, and
    b. any rewards (income to the system) accruing from the prospective need reduction will be equitably distributed among the members.

5. Perception of the appropriateness of the probable emotional interchange between the consultant and the members of the system, in terms of the criteria that

    a. the members do not become so dependent that they will not be able to work without consultative support, and
    b. the members do not become so hostile toward or frightened by the dependency involved in the consultation that the consultant cannot be constructively employed.

Each of the five dimensions carries its own dynamic for change. Need perceptions are never entirely satisfactory, and the search for "real" needs is perpetual. Role allocation can never truly fit the individual differences among people and the ever-changing requirements of the tasks of the system. Both formal and informal role reallocation is continuous and sometimes painfully slow. Resource distribution can never keep pace with changing needs nor reward distribution with the balance between needs and changing contributions (Parsons & Shils, 1952; Parsons, 1954). Finally, the exchange of feeling can never be all-supportive. Interdependencies always yield fears of dependency. Deprivation—even relative deprivation—yields apathy or rebellion. Evaluation yields fight and flight. Even support can yield jealousy. Any situation into which the consultant intervenes has its own dynamic for constructive changes and restraints (Lewin, 1947). The task is to find and reduce the restraining forces—liberating the growth potential of the system.

Variations in optimal conditions for entry

The foregoing outline of the significant conditions for entry were cast in terms of perceptions. One might construe this to mean that the optimal conditions for entry are those in which the perceptions of the consultant and those of the power centers of the system are in substantial agreement. Such a construction was not intended, and it seems unlikely that such a situation can ever be found. The entry of the consultant into the system implies more or less change in the system—resulting in part from the impact of the attachment of a new role to the old system of role, resource, and reward allocation. The question of optimal entry conditions involves estimates of the extent to which the consultant and the client system may hold congruent, complementary, or conflicting perceptions and change tendencies. Congruence implies almost no change; complementarity, slow change; and conflict implies fast change or fast termination of the attachment. The possible combinations of conditions are tremendously large, but most of them have likely been met somewhere else in the practice of the helping professions.

Consultation in conflict

Sometimes a consultant attaches to a social system that disagrees with her or him in all significant respects: about the existence of the need, about the internal availability of resources, about the consultant's resources, about the basis for role, resource, and reward allocation, and about the feelings appropriate in reaction to the consultant's efforts. The great tradition of the reformer carries with it the theme of consultation in conflict. The theme has had many variations, but the reforming consultant and the client system have often differed most sharply in their perception of the proper locus of power. For example, Poston's work has been stimulated by a gnawing dissatisfaction with power vested in central control of material resources.

> Human values were lost in a maze of punch cards and number systems which were devoid of flesh and blood. Neighborhood life in any meaningful sense, the environment which had nurtured initiatives, civic integrity, and social responsibility, began

to grow sterile. The control which men had once exercised over their own lives gradually slipped away into distant offices of a centralized and impersonal society. (Poston, 1953, p. 6)

The consultant intended to alter the locus of power in the system and, consequently, the distribution of roles, resources, and rewards. The success of the first foray of such a reform movement depends in part upon the direction of changes already under way in the system and in part upon the availability of a subsystem ready to promote the reform. Taylor's dream of a "third force" of efficiency experts independent of both labor and management lacked a power point of entry until it sold its independence to either management or labor (Taylor, 1911). Poston (1953) seeks his power point of entry in community organization of dormant leadership. His goal is to transfer power from existing "non-democratic" organizations to the new democratic community organization.

When clients resist consultation, some consultants have succeeded as methodologists who suggest and assist in the conduct of self-surveys or other interpretative appraisals by the client system. Attempts to provide interpretive consultation in conflict have produced some remarkable successes, as with the work of Jacques (1952) and the Tavistock Institute, and Lindemann (1957), Kline (1958), and their associates at Wellesley.

One can ask, quite justifiably, whether such change agents as Poston or especially Alinsky (1946) were acting in the consultant's role. A broad and vague area separates the consultant group from the assault force, but, differentiated or not, both must select carefully the point in the power structure at which they enter.

Entry in the dark

A consultant often enters a system without any information about the state of affairs within the system regarding the dimensions significant to entry. He or she must gather data while entering and must face the possibility that the need is not seen by the most powerful member; that the consultant role has no place in the correct perception of role, resource, and reward allocation; and that the typical emotional reaction to the prospect of the consultant role is one of hostility or fear or both. The entering consultant can assume that, in spite of manifest pleas for help, within the informal channels of communication in the client system, many members are committed individually to a different diagnosis, doctor, and treatment plan.

The observation phase

Can a prospective consultant take a properly humble posture? Perhaps. He can propose that a provisional relationship be established, enabling him to study the client system and enabling the system to study him. His "entry" is thus confined to the observer role. Observation surely threatens the system, but it is less potent than the active consultant role. And the system is invited to make the observation a two-way activity; the consultant withholds no information from any members who could be affected by the problem (so far as he knows). If such a temporary arrangement can be made, data can be collected to provide an estimate of whether any active entry can be made at all, and, if so, at what time and place in the system. Where negative indications are found, a constructive withdrawal is presumably possible.

Congruent need perception

A consultant or a client may think that a minimum requirement for entry is the mutual recognition of the need and its importance. Working on the congruence alone as a base for entry, the consultant will undertake—after an observation phase—a trial period of active consultation. He or she will propose that the trial period will reveal, first, whether the needed resources are available within the system. If they are found, the relationship can be curtailed and gradually terminated. If they are not found, the consultant's own skills can be tested for quality. The distribution of the consultants services among the members of the system can be evaluated from time to time and modified to meet agreed-upon requirements for equity. In a like manner, the equity of the distribution of other resources and rewards can be ensured, with particular attention to the separation of the consultant's and the executive's roles. Finally, the feelings of the members about the consultant's activities can be assessed and, when it seems appropriate, interpreted to the members of the system.

This experimental period is much like the "pilot run" proposed by the Tavistock group (Jacques, 1947), but it differs in that it provides a more extensive period of experimentation. It runs through a series of phases but never really ceases to maintain its experimental orientation, particularly where the consultant-trainer role is required (Thelan, 1954).

The crux of the experimental approach is the initial agreement between the consultant and the power figures of the system on the criteria and the rules of evidence by which the experimental results are to be evaluated. Such an agreement may or may not entail a congruence of ultimate values; it must entail agreement on methods and immediate goals.

In developing mental health consultant-trainer roles in public schools, the St. Louis County group began with observation, used a series of conferences to explore perceptions of needs and definition of roles, and to develop a provisional action plan, with a "built-in" evaluation technique. The results were a program with steady growth but a wide variation in need perception, consultant-role definition, and action plans, including, in a few cases, the withdrawal of the consultant (Buchmueller & Domke, 1956; Gildea et. al., 1958; and Glidewell, 1955).

Congruent need and role perceptions

A less adventurous consultant will want not only an agreed-upon need, but also an authoritative establishment of the need for and acceptability of his role as consultant and the client's role. Resistance to consultation often results from the feeling of the executive that she "ought to" be able to solve the problem without consultation. The executive fears a successful solution by consultation because it could discredit her competence. The establishment and acceptance of the complementary consultation roles can neutralize such a source of resistance.

Given the agreement upon need and role allocation as a basis for entry (this assures the rate of the fee if not its cumulative amount), the consultant and the client system will try to agree upon a series of experiments with resources and reward distribution. Again, the necessary time investment must be made to reach initial agreement on experimental methods and evaluative criteria.

Base and experimentation

A consultant may seek more and more congruence and leave less and less to experimentation, but at least two limits appear. The consultant who expects fully to ensure appropriate and realistic interchange of feelings between herself and the members asks for some rather unusual advantages. She asks for valid and reliable data about the feelings of persons, and this is hard to come by. She also asks that both the client system and she resolve their conflicts about authority and dependency before she enters. Ten years of human relations training and research and experience by the National Training Laboratories (NTL Institute) has reaffirmed the significance of dependency conflicts, but it has also established the difficulty of resolving them (e.g., Stock & Thelen, 1958).

A second limit is set by the strength of values upon progress and change. At least in western civilization (and certainly in modern India and China) the value set on progress is as strong as the resistance to change. The more the congruence of perception needed by the consultant as a basis for entry, the fewer are the opportunities for change. Most consultants try to strike a balance between an assaultive consultation in conflict and a pedestrian consultation in comfort.

There are, of course, all sorts of possible combinations of agreement and experimentation. Role, resource, and reward distributions often get established before there is an agreement about the nature of the problem. Data collection follows. Sometimes constructive emotional interchanges emerge first and substantive experimentation follows. The situations are as varied as life.

The consultant is often admonished to enter "at the top" of the power structure, but, as has been pointed out (e.g., Demerath, 1952), in complex organizations many "tops" may provide points of entry. The combinations and permutations of wholes and parts of a social system present infinite variety.

Experimentation is uncertain, costly in time and work, and provisional even in its outcome. Judgment about entry is a matter of calculated risk. Knowledge of the dimensions of the problem aid in the calculation.

Summary

I have suggested that the entry problem can be defined in terms of the goodness of fit (in congruence, complementarity or conflict) between the consultant and the client social system with respect to three principal variables:

1. perception of need;
2. perception of prospective equity of role, resource, and reward distribution; and
3. perception of prospective appropriateness of emotional interchange, with special concern about dependency and counterdependency.

References

Alinsky, S.D. *Reveille for radicals.* Chicago: University of Chicago Press, 1946.

Buchmueller, A.D., & Domke, II, R. The role of the public health department in preventive mental health services. *Children,* 1956, *3,* 225-31.

Demerath, N.J. Initiating and maintaining research relations in military organization. *Journal of Social Issues,* 1952, *8,* 11-23.

Festinoer, L., & Kelly, H.H. *Changing attitudes through social contact.* Ann Arbor: Research Center for Group Dynamics, University of Michigan, 1951.

Gildea, M.C.L. Community mental health research: Findings after three years. *American Journal of Psychiatry,* 1958, *114*(11), 970-976.

Glidewell, J.C. An experimental mental health program in Webster Groves. In *Third Yearbook, American Association of Public Schools.* New York: Columbia University, 1955.

Henry, J. *Concepts of social structure and personalization.* Unpublished manuscript, Washington University, St. Louis, Mo. 1959.

Jacques, E. (Ed.). Social therapy. *Journal of Social Issues,* 1947, *3* (2), 1-66.

Klein, D.C., & Ross, A. Kindergarten entry: A study of the role transition. In M. Krugman (Ed.), *Orthopsychiatry and the School.* New York: American Orthopsychiatric Association, 1958.

Lewin, K. Frontiers in group dynamics. *Human Relations,* 1947, *1,* 5-41.

Lindemann, E. *Mental health in the classroom: The Wellesley experience.* A paper presented at the annual meeting of the American Psychological Association, New York, 1957.

Lippitt, R., Watson, J., & Westley, B. *The dynamics of planned change.* New York: Harcourt, Brace & Company, 1958.

Mann, F.C., & Lippitt, R. (Eds.). Social skills in field research. *Journal of Social Issues,* 1952, *8,* (3) 1-50.

Parsons, T., & Shils, E.A. (Eds.). *Toward a general theory of action.* Cambridge: Harvard University Press, 1952.

Parsons, T. (Ed.), *Essays in sociological theory.* Glencoe, Ill.: The Free Press, 1954.

Poston, R.W. *Small town renaissance.* New York: Harper, 1950.

Poston, R.W. *Democracy is you.* New York: Harper, 1953.

Stock, D., & Thelen, H.A. *Emotional dynamics and group culture.* Washington, D.C.: National Training Laboratories, 1953.

Taylor, F.W. *The principles of scientific management.* New York: Harper, 1911.

Thelen, H.A. *The dynamics of groups at work.* Chicago: University of Chicago Press, 1954.

Client/Consultant Contact Problems

Arthur M. Freedman

Courtship rituals and trust building

No one enjoys revealing the discomfort or alarm caused by unsatisfactory conditions in work life. Yet when clients confront themselves with consultants, particularly when these change-agents are strangers, the obvious task is that of self-disclosure.

The first contact a consultant has with a prospective client system may be through a single representative, or a small group of self-appointed or delegated representatives who may or may not reflect the heterogeneity of the entire client system, or a person—usually a senior line manager or staff specialist—who is not directly involved in the work life of the client system.

Most representatives of client systems have experienced increasing dissatisfaction and frustration over an extended period. Such unpleasant feelings derive from either chronic or increasing discrepancies between perceived "existing" versus "desired" conditions of work. Over time, if one develops no changes in view, anxiety, tension, resentment, bitterness, and anger merge and complicate the work environment.

Feeling somewhat responsible, the spokesperson for the client system often presents the perceived problem in a somewhat distorted or incomplete manner. The intent seems to be to avoid personal responsibility, to avoid being blamed. People often attribute problems to "events," "conditions," or to some aspect of their organization's "environment." Distortions and selective omissions are complicated by the reality that no person, subgroup, or class of people can be aware of all aspects of any given problem situation. Their perspectives are individual and limited: each person and subgroup who is affected by the problem perceives and comprehends only some of the manifestations and ramifications of the problem.

The consultant must *know* that he or she cannot get the entire picture from initial meetings with a single spokesperson or even a homogeneous subgroup.

The event of initial contact is like a blind date. Both consultant and, particularly, the client or spokesperson feels concerned about the possibility of being misunderstood, blamed, exploited, or injured—inadvertently or otherwise. Therefore, as with blind dates, a certain amount of testing, back and forth, tends to occur. Through this process some form of a relationship is initiated. Depending upon how the consultant manages the interactions, this event can be the occasion of the creation of a foundation upon which trust can be built.

A form of courtship can begin if all parties agree to a trial period or small pilot project as a basis for exploring a possible consultant relationship. Such a courtship provides the consultant with opportunities to establish relationships with all affected subgroups within the client system and to clarify mutual expectations, assess the client system members' readiness to change, and clarify the nature of the consultant's role.

Who is the client?

When making initial contact, the consultant experiences difficulty in determining whether an administrator, for example, speaks for the total organization, some special interest subgroup, or only on behalf of his or her own vested interests. Unless the consultant conceives of the total organization as the client, he or she becomes vulnerable to being trapped into a special relationship with one subgroup or client-system member. When perceived by the rest of the client system, the consultant is likely to experience considerable difficulty in establishing open, productive relationships with other subgroups and with the total client system.

One way of focusing the issue is to consider the functional roles assumed by a different subgroups and individuals within the client system:

a. *the target*, which is a designated individual or subgroup whose behavior or style of functioning is perceived as problematic or as a source of discomfort by

b. *the beneficiaries* or other subgroups or individuals with whom "the target" is interdependent and whose support and/or contributions are highly valued by

c. *the managerial sponsors*, who occupy the positions of legitimate authority and power within a subsystem of the larger organization or at the top of the total organization and who, in response to "the beneficiaries' " requests for help, recruit, authorize, and subsidize

d. *the consultant* who is the internal or external professional helper or change-agent whose mandated responsibility is to intervene upon "the target" individual or subgroup in behalf of "the sponsor" acting in the perceived interest of "the beneficiaries."

The sequence is illustrated in Figure 1.

Establishing contact with the "whole" client system often requires working closely with representative task-force groups composed of spokespersons from all functional work units and role subgroups. Through such task forces, channels for two-way communication are created and kept open to all subgroups in the client system and between all such subgroups.

Figure 1
Sequence of actions and actors in consultative process

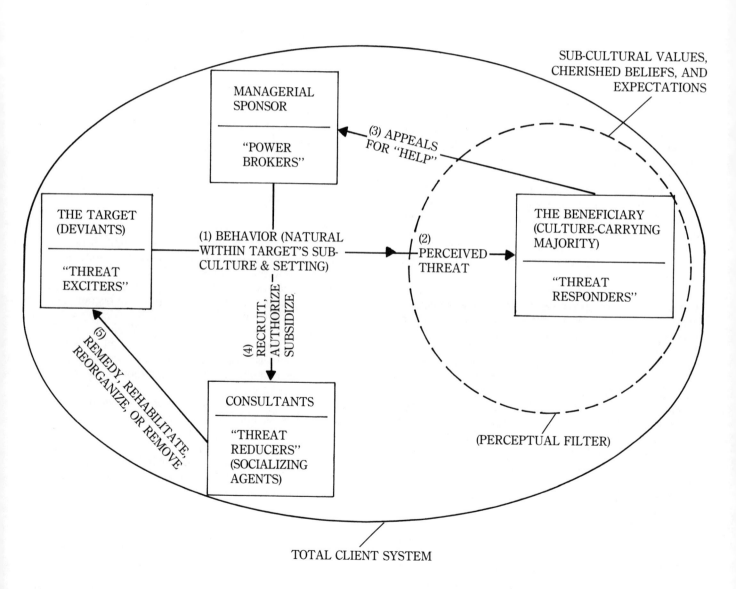

Limited purposes (instrumental objectives)

To achieve the terminal objective of client-system self-reliance, the initial contact must be managed in such a way as to achieve at least five limited, instrumental objectives. These "building blocks" are

Mutual understanding

—The consultant comprehends—and provisionally accepts—the client-system spokesperson's perceptions of the problem situation(s).
—The client representative comprehends—and provisionally accepts—the consultant's methods and values.

Mutual expectations

Client representative and consultant discuss, explore, and hammer out differences and agree—at least provisionally—to acceptable answers to such questions as

—"What are the objectives of the planned change?"
—"How will the planned change process work?"
—"What specific functions and tasks will have to be performed?"
—"Who will be responsible for which functions?"
—"What resources will be required—e.g., people, skills, knowledge, time, money, materials, supplies, equipment, facilities?"

Mutual commitment (contract)

A formal working agreement can be consumated prior to initial contact, upon the conclusion of these initial interactions, or after (as a result of) a pilot project or a trial period.
—The consultant decides that he or she is willing to work with the client system.
—The client's sponsors decide they are willing to invest the necessary agreed-upon resources—including their own active participation.
—The client's members who will be affected by the planned change decide they are willing to participate.

Initial next steps

—Validate or modify original assessment of client's problem situations—i.e., tap into all parts of system.
—Rank problems; obtain authorization.
—Set specific, measurable change objective(s).
—Plan initial change efforts.
—Implement, monitor, evaluate impact of initial plans.
—Continue and expand consultation—or terminate it.

Anxiety management

—The client-system representatives' anxiety and tension must be reduced to the degree that they are willing to disclose their perceptions of the problem without defensiveness, distortion, and omissions.
—The consultant's anxiety and tension must be reduced to the degree that he or she can perceive maximum comprehension and minimal distortions, omissions, or attributions.

Consider what the consultant risks:

—prestige, status, reputation;
—current and future income;
—opportunity to achieve, fail, violate one's own ethics;
—criticism, blame, self-esteem.

Consider what the client system risks:

—poor investment of scarce organizational resources (benefits less than costs);
—an open "can of worms" consultation evolving beyond intended limits, "sensitive" issues prematurely illuminated;
—criticism or blame directed toward parts of client system by other subgroups or consultant (or stockholders);
—the consultant may sound good but be incompetent ("false positive") or may sound poor but be effective ("false negative").

Games people play

Too often "game-like" situations are created within the client-consultant relationship which threaten or prevent constructive progress. These games, according to Pinkerton, Miller & Martin may be initiated by either the client or consultant and are based upon "poorly understood communications and, frequently, as a result of unconscious motivation" (p. 14).

Some illustrative games which consultants may "play" are

—"You [client] try to figure out what I [consultant] am supposed to be doing here."
—"Let's not really define the problem" or "I [consultant] will only look at the presenting problem—or the designated problem-creator(s)."
—"I [consultant] am the expert."
—"I [consultant] am only trying to help you [client]."

Some of the client-system members' favorite games are

—"You [consultant] tell us what to do—even though we already have the knowledge, skills, and experiences."
—"Join us in our misery and our gripe sessions."
—"It's not our fault, we [clients] inherited problems

which were created by other people or conditions over which we have no control.''
—"You [consultant] don't really understand the situation.''

Consultants may fall into such traps by assuming the requested help is really wanted; the intellectual and emotional components of the client's description of the focal problem situation are consonant; and a problem situation, once defined, is also clarified.

Clients may impede the development of productive consultative relationships also by assuming:

—The consultant will immediately grasp the essentials of the problem situation—he or she can both read minds and predict the future.
—The consultant will provide a simple solution or formula which will not disturb the preferred habit patterns of the members of the client system and will require little expenditure of resources (the most important of which are time and energy).
—The consultant can make the problem situation disappear alone, without disturbing the client-system members who are using their time dealing with their day-to-day routines.

Such assumptions, being essentially incompatible with the theory and methods of process consultation, form the foundations for disappointment, frustration, and anxiety. Client and consultant "games" tend to grow in fertile but counterproductive emotional environments.

Effective consulting relationships

Criteria for predicting "good" (low) consultation risks are the following:

—Clients are willing to assume responsibility for managing their organizational problems.
—Clients have a history of establishing functional and effective working relationships with others.
—Clients do not project or attribute the causes of their problems or the reasons for their perpetuation to other people, past history, or impersonal environmental factors.
—Clients do not seek inappropriate dependency relations.

Taking care to minimize risk by employing these criteria, consultants might educate their clients by

—Specifying the consultant's intent to work toward enabling client-system members to become self-reliant.
—Negotiating a mutually acceptable working agreement (or contract) which specifies both consultant's and client-system members' obligations.

If, in spite of all precautions, deviations from the intent of the working agreement begin to evolve, either the client or consultant might initiate the following corrective methods:

—One may re-examine, clarify, and renegotiate the original working agreement, objectives, and purposes.
—Particularly when client subgroups or individuals begin to behave in a dysfunctionally anxious or excessively defensive manner as a result of high stress, consultants may have to halt the planned change effort temporarily to provide and help clients learn how and when to provide mutual support.
—Direct, nonjudgmental feedback from consultant to client (or from one client to another with the assistance of the consultant) regarding how the other's behavior is perceived and responded to when that behavior is experienced as dysfunctional. To make sure that such feedback is helpful in situations characterized by confusion, frustration, impatience, and pessimism, the giver of feedback may wish to add, "And, I want you to. . . (act some specific different way)." The giver of feedback should make some legitimate request. Naturally, the consultant will have already coached client-system members in the use of affirming and appreciative feedback prior to the emergence of the need for corrective feedback. Being familiar with the more "positive" form, clients are less reluctant to employ the more "critical" version.

Reference

Pinkerton, Miller, & Martin. Consultation—Or how we wile away the hours. *Professional Psychology*, 1974, *5*(1), 13-17.

Client Contact: Entry and Contract

Marvin R. Weisbord

Components of a good, supportive contract include

Clarity of responsibilities

a) Who is the client?

b) Who (client or consultant) shall contact the *(entry)* other members of the system and what will they be told?

c) What will be the responsibilities of the *(contract)* consultant?
   1. data collection *(consultant*
   2. analysis *responsibilities)*
   3. feedback
   4. recommendations
   5. follow-up

d) What will be the responsibilities of the client? *(client*
   1. expectations held about consultant *concerns)*
   2. confidentiality
   3. How will data be used?
   4. Who will be involved in the feedback?
   5. Are reports (written or oral) needed?
   6. Is "follow-up" expected?

e) How do you know you have completed the task? *(closure)*
   1. When will the task be considered finished"? *(mutual*
   2. Will there be an evaluation and, if so, when? *concern)*
   3. Who is responsible for an evaluation?
   4. What are the projected costs and how will they be paid?

Clean contract

When the conditions of the working relationship are understood and accepted by all persons involved, when there is an agreement to renegotiate with an equality of power and concern; when there is a mutually accepted responsibility to discuss all concerns openly, a clean contract results.

© Marvin R. Weisbord. Used by permission.

Contracting

The nature of contracting:

1. Repetitive process (constant revision, renewal, extension to more people and groups)
2. Task, where underlying process is critical

Functions of contracting:

1. Sets mutual expectations
2. Creates needed structure for relationship (forces choices of game plan from unlimited possibilities)
3. Creates hope
4. Establishes ground rules for behavior: anonymity of data; whole system as client; mutual feedback; legitimacy of differences, conflict
5. Names goals and incentives for both parties

Content issues:

1. Client's view of problem
2. Do consultant's skills fit?
3. Logistics of first event: people, length of time, dates, nature of design
4. Procedures consultant will follow; time demands on clients, costs
5. Hoped-for *observable* outcomes (How will client *know* the system is improving?)
6. Who will do what?

Process issues:

1. Does the client like me [the consultant]? And do I like the client?
2. Will client accept some responsibility for problem?
3. Is the client open with me? I with the client? Is the client open to new data from others?
4. Anxiety over risk?
5. Can we talk about process in this interview and deal with it successfully?

How to connect with clients:

1. reflect, empathize with strong feelings;
2. relate experiences elsewhere, names of other clients;

3. talk about both failures and successes;
4. state what you *can't* do;
5. state your values, concerning feedback, client's freedom of choice, and so forth;
6. discuss how your skill fits the client's concerns;
7. discuss the cost as investment (time and money)—only the client can decide if potential payoff is great enough;
8. ask the client to diagram the organization, list people key to change effort, and so forth;
9. list pros and cons of proceeding; and
10. avoid jargon, focus on the *client's* content issues.

Risks:

1. promising too much, creating unrealistic expectations;
2. failing to act on uneasiness in discussion;
3. appearing to accept the client's definition of problem as valid for all rather than just for that individual;
4. the person may not have final authority to hire; and
5. the client is window-shopping, not seriously interested in hiring a consultant.

Objectives of first meeting (in order of importance):

1. firm contract for Intervention X: dates selected, price agreed upon, client liaison named, tasks of each party made clear;
2. Intervention X tentative, dates to be decided, letter or phone call needed to firm up;
3. details clear, proposal to be written then followed up;
4. client really not a client yet—door open for return visit; and
5. meeting was a mistake; person not a potential client, now or ever. Do I know why?

A strong contract is characterized by the following:

1. high commitment from the person with power to make a contract;
2. personal involvement from the person with power to make a contract;
3. committed internal liaison or consultant;
4. budget clear, not a major issue;
5. dates selected, persons to be involved chosen;
6. objectives clear;
7. consultant and client both have good feelings about each other;
8. anxieties discussed openly;
9. possible risks discussed openly;
10. step is diagnostic, or based on previous diagnosis with people who will participate.

A weak contract is characterized by the following:

1. consultant has uneasy feelings, not sure why;

2. client's ability to invest time is unclear;
3. organization under numerous other stresses (intervention has low priority);
4. inadequate planning time before event;
5. unclear relationship between internal and external consultant;
6. client abdicates all responsibility to consultant.

NOTE: A STRONG CONTRACT IS CENTRAL TO SUCCESS.

Contract check list

Process side

1. Feelings about own handling of sessions: Okay ____   Not Okay ____

2. Feelings about client   Okay ____   Not Okay ____

3. Any important "unfinished business"?
                                  Yes ____   No ____

Nature:

4. If "yes," what did you do about it?

5. How clear do you judge the client's understanding was of what you would and would not do?

     Very ____   Not Very ____   Not at All ____

6. How clear would you judge your understanding of the client's sense of risk and payoff?

     Very ____   Not Very ____   Not at All ____

7. What, if anything, would you do differently?

Content side

1. How explicit was the "frame" around your contract, i.e., time required, costs, what each person would have to do?

     Very ____   Not Very ____   Not at All ____

2. Where were you strongest in this contract?

3. Where weakest?

4. Did you introduce any exercises, events, or activities that came as a big surprise?

Yes _____   No _____

What happened?

5. How, if at all, would you change this contract now?

Two sample contracts

Contract in the form of a letter

Dear _____:

This will confirm our discussion of last Monday. As I understand it, you want to begin a more intensive development activity with your managers. We agreed that a short off-site workshop for the top team should be the first step. The objectives would be to

— clarify your expectations and goals for people reporting to you;
— ditto for their expectations of you;
— more clearly define relationships between line and staff managers, including ways they can help each other;
— develop a work plan for the top team (i.e., frequency of meetings, agenda, action plans between meetings);
— examine ways to improve communication, decision-making, problem-solving skills of top team;
— provide support and ideas to your vice-presidents for developing their own staff and management teams.

I propose the entire team be involved in setting the agenda for the workshop. I will conduct a one-hour interview with each person. Questions might include those on the attached list, plus others to be worked out between us. All responses will be combined anonymously into a diagnostic report. Only items approved by each participant will be included. The report will be given out at the start of the workshop.

My role will be to help you identify high-priority agenda items and consult with you and your team as you work on them. I will also be ready to introduce specific procedures should the interview data suggest that would be helpful. The final format would be based on a discussion of the data between you and me on the day the workshop is to begin.

I propose we start on Wednesday afternoon and run through Friday afternoon, with work sessions both evenings. This will give us a solid 2½ days. Interviews, preparation of report, and the design and implementation of the workshop will require six days of my time at a cost of $_____ plus expenses.

I look forward to working with you.

Sincerely,

Contract in the form of a memo

Contract Between Department of _____ and Marvin Weisbord

Objective: Diagnosis and action plan to improve departmental organization

1. Chairman will name 10-12 department members who represent emerging administrative structure.

2. A two-day meeting in January will have as its purposes

   a. joint diagnosis of the existing situation, both structure and behavior;
   b. beginning of formation of an administrative team to work together on a reorganization.

3. Clients agree to open discussion of any matter relevant to departmental administration.

4. Consultant agrees to facilitate discussion, to see to it that all points of view are heard, and to help clients confront choices and dilemmas.

5. Consultant agrees to supply relevant methodology and theory in pursuit of objectives of meeting.

6. Consultant agrees to help the administrative group develop its own internal consultant if that seems desirable.

7. Client will handle all logistics and communications, i.e., setting up a site, informing participants, sending out advance agenda, taking notes during meeting, typing up and distributing to all any diagnostic data and/or decisions reached during each meeting.*

8. The initial meeting will involve Marvin and one colleague, at a cost of $_____ plus expenses.

9. Whether to have further meetings will be a joint decision of client and consultant after the initial event.

*Consultant will treat all information as confidential. It is up to the client to decide who should receive what information.

Practical Issues on Data Gathering Within the Process Consulting Effort

Arthur M. Freedman

Regardless of the diagnostic model used, or the types of data collected, or the sources of that data, or the specific methods by which the data was obtained, the sooner that data is fed back into the system, the smoother the consultative process will evolve. Long delays between data collection and feedback usually cause heightened anxiety, frustration, resentment, and anger on the part of the providers of information. Data gathering is a consultative intervention: when information is collected about particular issues, providers tend to expect that "something" will be done by "someone." Usually, data providers hold top management "responsible." If too much time elapses before information providers see evidence of some kind of response, awkward organizational situations may become either quagmires of pessimism and apathy or arenas for revolts.

Process consultation differs from the medical model of technical expert consultation in two ways: the process consultant does not make self-authorized diagnoses nor prescribe recommended solutions and the process consultant feeds the organized (according to the diagnostic model) data back to those who provided the information in the first place. The notion is that data providers own the data and, since they are likely to be involved or affected by any planned change effort, they are entitled to participate in making decisions about diagnosis, priorities, change objectives, action plans, and implementation.

Since anyone is entitled to attempt to focus attention on any data collected, top management of the client system must be prepared—and willing—to act on anything about which questions have been asked, regardless of how "sensitive" such issues may be. Therefore, prior to data collection, consultants should examine each question or topic area in light of this consideration: "Should this issue turn out to be a key problem, are we prepared and willing to focus on it?" If not, they must delete questions pertaining to the "sensitive" issue. Otherwise, consultants will have allowed client-system members to start a game of organizational "Russian Roulette." Keep this axiom in mind: "Don't pull the pin until you are ready to throw the grenade."

Diagnosis *Is* an Intervention

ROBERT J. LEE AND IRVIN ROBINSON

The word "diagnosis," usually associated with medical practice, means "to understand or know the underlying reasons or causes" for something. We use the word in OD and consulting, along with other words from the same sources—such as "intervention"—but with somewhat different intentions.

A medical doctor diagnoses the patient *before* taking any actions to help. The process consultant typically has few, if any, opportunities to do this, and generally does not want to. Most of the diagnostic process must and should be a participative learning experience for the client. The diagnostic process is itself a series of interventions and should be seen as an integral part of the helping process. The obvious paradox is that the client and process consultant are trying to figure what to do *while* actually doing things that have a significant impact on the client. Imagine what would happen if the acts of taking X-rays and blood samples changed what the X-rays and lab results eventually showed.

In some ideal world, or perhaps in some simple medical situations, one could hope to observe the client objectively, gather data, come to a diagnosis, plan an intervention, and arrange for it to be implemented—all without there being any change in the client. In the organizational world, however, such is not the case. Often it is also not the case in medicine, either—for example, a person's blood pressure may change just because his or her blood pressure is being checked.

Diagnosis in process consulting is a complex, interactive event. It creates certain inevitable interventions into the client system. These interventions are extended even further if the consultant takes certain optional actions as part of the diagnosis phase of consulting. The result is that by the time the consultant and the client agree on a desired planned intervention, the client is no longer quite the same as when it all began. The client is now one who has participated in a successful diagnostic process and has learned something from it. That learning is a by-product of the diagnostic process.

For the process-oriented consultants, the model might look like the chart in Figure 1. Both the ideal and the actual situations start with some kind of reality—a real person or social system. Also, both situations end up with

a modified reality. But that is where the analogy ends. Actions that belong wholly to the doctor in the simplified medical model are shared by the client and consultant in the organizational setting. Mutual influence and impact are inevitable at each step, beginning with the decisions to ask for help and to offer help.

Organizational filters exist which magnify the apparent importance of some aspects of the reality, while simultaneously blurring or totally obscuring other aspects. The organization selects, consciously or otherwise, only certain parts of itself to show the consultant. This happens for many reasons, including desires to look good or to complain, the specific reasons for having an interest in a consultant's help, who the consultant is and how the consultant happened to be chosen. For example, a black and/or female consultant may receive a version of reality different from the one given to a white male consultant. Distortion is inevitable, however, since any client system is too complex to be seen in its entirety.

Consultants may find it a useful practice to "check out" whether or not an important organizational filter is operating. Some questions might be "Why are you telling me about this so soon?", "It's interesting that you hadn't shown me this side of the group process earlier," or "Is this the way things usually happen?" Of course, the decision to "check out" an organizational filter is itself an intervention.

The data gathering and observation activity is shared by both parties. The mere presence of the consultant creates a change in the normal state of affairs, and is therefore an intervention, too. Clients are asked unusual questions or are observed in special meetings. These questions, answers, interviews, and meetings provide data for the consultant but, because of the extraordinary situation, they become data for the clients as well. In this sense, data is not just observed, but is first generated in a visible, participatory way and then jointly observed.

The consultant's own filters are easily overlooked because they usually operate unconsciously. Like the organizational filters, they give prominence or anonymity to data, or lead to other distortions. These filters arise out of the consultant's needs and background. Imagine, for example, how differently two consultants would interpret observed data if one were a Marxist and the other a right-wing political reactionary. Or if one were

Figure 1
Diagnostic Model for Process Oriented Consultants

Client's Actions/Status	Consultant's Actions/Status	Process/Comment
1. Initial "real" situation; request for help	Agreement to give help	Essential step; creates by-product intervention (client feels less alone, better, threatened, successful, or whatever)
2. Organizational filtering; respond to consultant	"Check out" nature of filters	Optional step; creates by-product intervention (client learns about own filters)
3a. Respond to consultant and to own data as it is generated	Data gathering and observation	Essential step; creates by-product intervention (client discovers what's important to consultant and may react to own response)
3b. Respond to consultant	Consultant's filtering; "check out" nature of filters	Optional step; creates by-product intervention (client learns about how consultant thinks, feels, values)
3c.	Categorizing of data	
4.	Attempts at agreement with self and team	
5. Data display and attempts at agreement on a diagnosis by all concerned; if successful,* then proceed to Step 6		Essential step; creates by-product interventon (client learns about itself, how to interpret data, sharing, etc.)
6. Jointly plan and implement an intervention appropriate to sanctioned diagnosis		Intentional (*vs.* by-product) intervention
7. Resulting "real" situation		

*If unsuccessful, then either (A) recycle to earlier step or (B) exit. Either of these becomes an important intervention.

interested in research and the other in social action. Or if one were a clinical psychologist and the other a personnel generalist. Some of these filters represent areas of self-interest which may be shared with the client. Doing so is a way to "check out" these interests, and this act represents another intervention into the client system.

Consultants usually have their own **priority categories**—things they like to look for, areas of activity that are meaningful to them. Leadership styles, climate, decision making, sexism, control systems, affect legitimacy, and so forth. Process consultants have their favorites and tend to change their favorites from time to time. No one can interpret all of the data in terms of all of the possible categories, and no list of categories is ever perfect.

These three topics—data observation, consultant's filters, and priority categories—tend to occur simultaneously. Describing them separately and in sequence is convenient, but it does not reflect how it happens. The numbering of these steps (3a, b, c) on the model in Figure 1 reflects their concurrent timing.

At some point, however, the consultant has as much data as he or she wants. There is a step in which a test is made as to whether the variety, consistency, reliability, and scope of data are sufficient. When a consultant works alone, this step may occur silently or quickly. When a consulting team is working, the **agreement-testing** process is much more evident. Depending on the prevailing OD theory being used, more or less interpretation of the data may be attempted at this point.

The next step is **data display** and working with the client to agree that the data are useful and sufficient for jointly developing a **diagnosis**. This step clearly is an intervention by the consultant into the client system, even though diagnosis is a decision as to how and when to intervene.

If agreement cannot be reached, then the consultant has two choices:

- *go back*, with the client, to an earlier step to check on filters, to re-categorize the data, or to gather more data, perhaps using a more explicit or a different approach; or

- *exit* from the client system by acknowledging a mismatch, lack of skill, unreadiness, or other reason for this not being a right combination of time, people, and circumstances.

If agreement on "a diagnosis" is reached, an **intervention** can be planned and implemented. The outcome is a modified reality, and the cycle may or may not have a need to repeat.

Some Characteristics of Static vs. Innovative Organizations*
MALCOLM S. KNOWLES

DIMENSIONS	CHARACTERISTICS	
	Static Organizations	Innovative Organizations
Structure	Rigid—much energy given to maintaining permanent departments, committees; reverence for tradition, constitution and by-laws Hierarchical—adherence to chain of command Roles defined narrowly Property-bound	Flexible—much use of temporary task-forces; easy shifting of departmental lines; readiness to change constitution, depart from tradition Multiple linkages based on functional collaboration Roles defined broadly Property-mobile
Atmosphere	Task-centered, impersonal Cold, formal, reserved Suspicious	People-centered, caring Warm, informal, intimate Trusting
Management Philosophy and Attitudes	Function of management is to control personnel through coercive power Cautious—low risk-taking Attitude toward errors: to be avoided Emphasis on personnel selection Self-sufficiency—closed system regarding sharing resources Emphasis on conserving resources Low tolerance for ambiguity	Function of management is to release the energy of personnel; power is used supportively Experimental—high risk-taking Attitude toward errors: to be learned from Emphasis on personnel development Interdependency—open system regarding sharing resources High tolerance for ambiguity
Decision making and Policy making	High participation at top, low at bottom Clear distinction between policy making and policy execution Decision making by legal mechanisms Decisions treated as final	Relevant participation by all those affected Collaborative policy making and policy execution Decision making by problem solving Decisions treated as hypotheses to be tested
Communication	Restricted flow—constipated One-way—downward Feelings repressed or hidden	Open flow—easy access Multidirectional—up, down, sideways Feelings expressed

*Reprinted from *The Modern Practice of Adult Education: From Pedagogy to Andagogy*, © 1980 Malcolm S. Knowles. Published by Cambridge, The Adult Education Company, 888 Seventh Avenue, New York, New York 10106. Reprinted by permission of the publisher.

Six-Box Diagnostic Model*

Marvin R. Weisbord

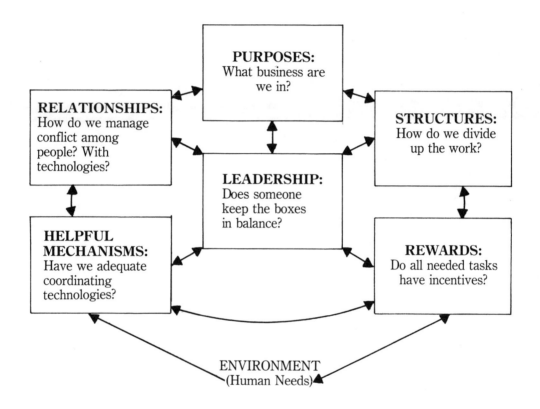

NOTE: The model can be seen as a radar screen. Organizational problems appear as "blips" of varying intensity. It is management's unending task to scan, assure balance among the boxes, identify and close gaps between "what is" and "what ought to be," between "what is produced," and "what should be produced." Leadership is responsible for providing a mechanism to maintain the scan. Moreover, closing a gap always requires the use of some helpful mechanism. Unless a mechanism exists or can be created, nothing is likely to happen.

Diagnostic tip: Identify the "missing pieces" in each box.

Organizational diagnostic model

1. The chart summarizes relationships among Purposes, Structure, Relationships, Rewards, Helpful Mechanisms, Leadership, Environmental Demands.

2. It assumes that Purposes will be related to Environ-

*From *Organizational Diagnosis: Six Places to Look for Trouble With or Without a Theory* by Marvin R. Weisbord, Addison Wesley, 1976. Used by permission.

mental demands—i.e., an organization's priorities should be based on what it *must* do to fulfill its mission at this time in this place.

3. Structure will be based on Purposes. In organizations, as in architecture, form follows function. For example, functional—or departmental—organization is a strong structure for developing in-depth special competence. It is much less effective in carrying out integrative projects. By contrast, a product—or program or project— organization is strong at coordinating around special

purposes, and pays for this through less in-depth specialized capability, such as production or sale.

Historically, organizations have reorganized periodically in one or the other mode as environment, technologies, and strategies changed. Where both capabilities are equally important, organizations—e.g., aerospace industry, medical schools—have gone to a matrix. This requires sophisticated conflict management.

4. Relationships refers primarily to the way units are coordinated. This is another way of saying "conflict management," for the critical problem in coordinating differentiated activities is managing inevitable conflict between them. The more complex—i.e., matrix-like—the required structure, the more conflict management becomes a critical requirement for effective organization.

5. Rewards help or inhibit the "fit" between individuals and organizational goals. Ideally, organizations should offer incentives—e.g., promotions, achievements, money—for people to do what most needs doing. In practice, reward systems sometimes work against the organization's best interest. Piecework incentive plans sometimes have this unintended consequence and, in medicine, academic promotion may hinge on research, even though a medical center is under pressure to teach and serve patients.

6. Cutting across all four issues—Purposes, Structure, Relationships, Rewards—is the notion of Helpful Mechanisms. These are procedures, policies, systems, forms, committees, agendas which contribute to appropriate Purposes, Structure, Relationships, and Rewards. An effective organization continually revises its mechanisms, eliminating some and adding others as the need arises. Whenever a "gap" between what is and what ought to be is identified, it is often discovered that no present mechanism exists to close it. Hence, the creation of new mechanisms is central to the identification and closing of gaps.

7. Only Leadership can scan the entire environment and act on behalf of the whole. This is the appropriate role for top administration—to keep the entire organization in balance, continually creating mechanisms to articulate Purposes (and change them as the environment changes), alter Structure, and provide for appropriate Relationships and Rewards.

8. The model provides a vocabulary and way of thinking about these issues.

A Diagnostic Model for Organizational Change: Where the Flexible Is Functional*

	FUNCTIONAL AND EFFECTIVE	DYSFUNCTIONAL/WITHOUT USEFUL PURPOSE
AMENABLE TO CHANGE	**I.** *Area of Low Anxiety and Maximum Health* Parts or aspects of the organization which are currently functioning at an optimal level, are amenable to (and do) change as called for by new demands, emergent needs and unanticipated changes in the organization's internal or external environments. For example, the Executive Director and top management staff are well trained in problem solving and are willing to examine their own decision making processes and procedures. (Particularly good with counter-dependent clients.)	**II.** *Area of Natural Targets for Planned Change* Parts or aspects of the organization which are not working well but are amenable to change in that the authority to make the choice as to whether conditions will be altered or perpetuated is vested in those personnel who are affected by those conditions. For example organizational norms and standards, communication channels and styles and allocation of job functions and responsibilities among staff members and/or between functional work units.

Movement from Area II to I is highly probable with planned change interventions.

Lack of attention to maintenance leads to reduced possibility for self-conscious change (a natural progression without planned change interventions).

NOT AMENABLE TO CHANGE	**III.** *Area of Stop-Gap Measures (Functional Fixedness)* Expedient action is taken to manage unexpected problems on a temporary basis, but is not replaced by more comprehensive and permanent solutions. Instead of being recognized as having only time-limited utility, they may become institutionalized. For example, the "Acting" Director, "temporary" buildings, "interim" policies, "temporary" committees ("task forces").	**IV.** *Area of Organizational Disasters* Parts or aspects of the organization which are neither effective nor amenable to change in that those who are affected by conditions have no legitimate authority to influence them. For example, policies, objectives or methods are unilaterally mandated by those who may be unfamiliar with actual organizational conditions (governance boards, vested interest groups, legislatures). This is particularly disruptive when those with the authority to impose are unresponsive to the reactions of those imposed upon.

Inflexibility leads to reduced levels of adequate functioning
(a natural progression without systematic, planned change interventions).

*Based on the article by Steve Ruma in *Social Change, 4*(4), 1974. © 1974. NTL Institute. Adapted by Arthur M. Freedman.

Types of planned change interventions, Areas I to IV

I. Area of low anxiety and maximum health

In collaboration with members of the client system, develop a list of well-functioning aspects of the organization. This will help the staff to get used to working with the model while insuring that time, energy and support will continue to be provided for these healthy organizational components.

II. Area of natural targets for planned change

A. Collaboratively list and rank (in terms of staff's "*readiness* to change") all organizational factors.

B. Rank all factors a second time (in terms of "what is *possible* to be changed").

C. Plan and implement (monitor and evaluate) change interventions.

III. Area of stop-gap measures (functional fixedness)

A. Collaboratively list all such organizational factors to highlight and clarify those characteristics which cannot be depended upon.

B. Help the client-system staff members decide (force the issue, if necessary) whether or not to risk the expenditure of scarce resources in an attempt to replace some or all of these stop-gap organizational elements.

IV. Area of organizational disasters

A. Collaboratively list all such factors to enable staff to focus their problem-solving efforts on

1. *Insulating* the relatively healthy, well-functioning parts of the organization from the malignant elements. Limit the spread of negative effects;

2. *Avoiding* and *drainage* of scarce resources and energy from relatively healthy areas to the disaster areas.

B. Refer this list to the policy-making levels of management.

Survey Data Feedback Approach to Consultation*

DAVID NADLER

A five-stage cycle of survey data feedback

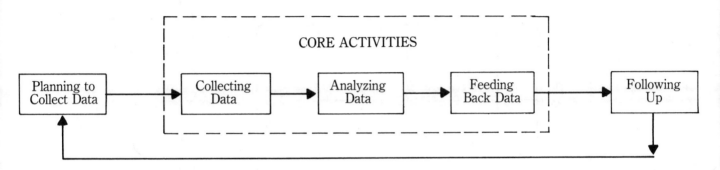

Comparison of Supervisory vs Consultant Feedback

Some examples of the five-stage cycle at the individual and group levels which Nadler provides are (p. 46):

SITUATION	SUPERVISOR CONDUCTS PERFORMANCE APPRAISAL	CONSULTANT WORKS WITH A GROUP
Planning to use data	Supervisor clarifies subordinate's functions, responsibilities, and goals. Sets "ground rules" for performance measurement and evaluation.	Group or team asks for help in working together. Group and consultant agree on the consultant's role.
Collecting data	Supervisor observes and records performance of subordinate.	Consultant observes interactions of group.
Analyzing data	Supervisor compares actual performance vs. standards and checks to see if conditions have changed.	Consultant compares actual process and attempts to identify patterns of behavior.
Feeding back data	Supervisor shares data and interpretations with subordinate. They discuss validity and implications of performance data.	Consultant describes aspects of group process as observed. Checks observations for accuracy and stimulates discussion or process issues.
Following up	Plans are jointly developed for remediation—training or new job assignments.	Consultant continues to work with group and helps group to develop its own capacity to observe and give feedback on its process.

*Excerpted from *Feedback and Organization Development: Using Data-based Methods*. Reading, MA: Addison-Wesley, 1977, pp. 43-44. Used by permission of David Nadler.

DYNAMICS OF DATA-BASED APPROACH TO O.D./PROCESS CONSULTATION*

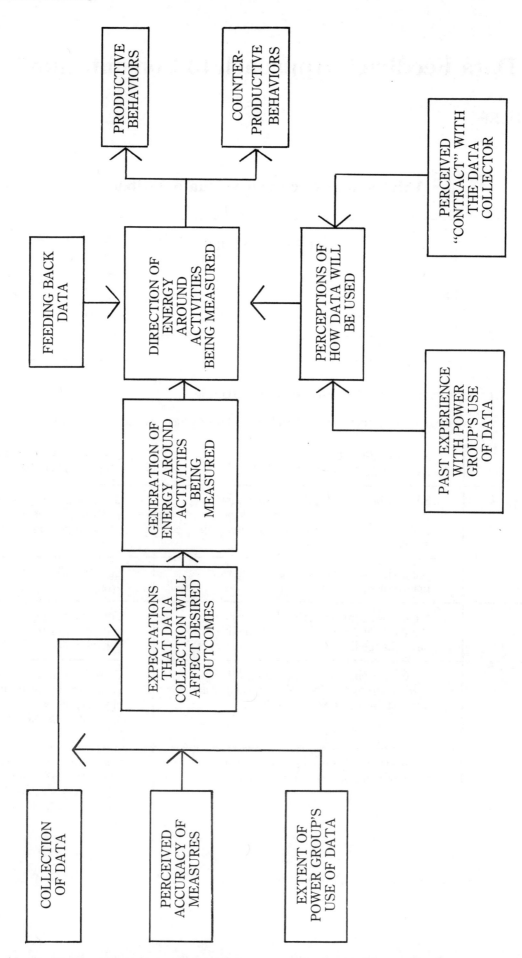

*Note that the process of collecting data *is* a consultative intervention in itself which will affect the members of the system from which data is gathered—regardless of method. This, in essence, is an example of the Heisenberg Principle (Ed.)

METHODS OF COLLECTING DATA

I. Interviews: individual or group
   openended
   semistructured
   structured

   A. Advantages
   1. Adaptive—data on large range of possible subjects
   2. Source of "rich" data
   3. Empathic—rapport-building

   B. Potential Problems
   1. Expensive
   2. Interviewer bias
   3. Coding/interpretation problems
   4. Self-report bias
   5. Retrospection
   6. Restricted to relatively small numbers

II. Questionnaires: standardized
   modified
   custom-made

   A. Advantages
   1. Quantifiable, easily summarized
   2. Useful with large numbers
   3. Relatively inexpensive
   4. Can obtain large volume of data
   5. Taps data client-system members may not have been aware of

   B. Potential Problems
   1. Nonempathic
   2. Predetermined questions may miss issues
   3. Overinterpretation
   4. Response bias
   5. Retrospection

III. Direct Observation
   A. Advantages
   1. Behavioral data, not reports of behavior
   2. Real time, not retrospective
   3. Adaptive
   4. Reveals data client-system members may not be aware of

   B. Potential Problems
   1. Interpretation/coding
   2. Sampling
   3. Observer bias/reliability
   4. Expense
   5. Heisenberg Principle

IV. Ratings (By peers, staff, bosses, subordinates, experts, clients, etc.)

V. MIS statistics/POMR

VI. Personal Diaries

VII. Clinical Exams

VIII. Physical Evidence (Nonobtrusive)

IX. Projective Tests

X. Simulations

XI. Tests of Specific Knowledge

Notes on Data Display and Feedback*

ALLAN DREXLER, MARVIN R. WEISBORD, AND PETER B. VAILL

Goals of a feedback meeting

(Call it "discussion," however, not feedback):

1. Present data.

2. Help participants own it.

3. Arrive at diagnosis of a few pertinent issues. For example, what accounts for gaps or variances that we can do something about?

4. Data reduction: focus on one, two, or three high-priority items.

5. Action steps: make a decision about what to do next on one, two, or three high-priority items.

6. Plan how to let others who supplied the data know what was found and what will be done about it.

Data display tips

1. KISS Principle (*K*eep *I*t *S*imple, *S*tupid)

2. Use clients' words whenever possible to cover main points. It takes little stimulus to get full range of data once the process starts.

3. Use simple models. The more you provide structure in advance, the harder it is for others to own data.

4. Data are stimulae for discussion and action. They are not by themselves a "diagnosis." The diagnosis comes only through discussion: assigning meaning to the words (based on a comprehensive and comprehensible diagnostic model).

5. Let clients wrestle with raw meanings before supplying your interpretation. You can always add it if nothing seems to happen.

*When the moment for data feedback arrives—the sooner after its collection, the better—consider the following "goals," "display tips" and "cautions"—Eds. (provided by: Allan Drexler, Marvin R. Weisbord, and Peter B. Vaill, NTL Con-skills lab, July 1974). Used by permission of Marvin R. Weisbord.

Cautions

1. Don't defend data. If people deny your data, ask them to supply the "real" data—here and now.

2. If necessary, throw away all data and let people make up a new set, on the spot.

3. Don't belabor issues past the point of ownership. When people say, "Yeah, that's us," it's time to consider what to do about it.

Comparing Successful and Unsuccessful OD Efforts*

PAUL BUCHANAN

1. Linkage between the target system and the larger system. An additional issue which is related to "linkage" is identification of the set of prevailing values in a component of an organization and determination of whether the values being introduced are compatible or competitive. When the values are compatible, the linkage problems would be less difficult than when they are competitive but such problems are not insurmountable in either case.

Changes are often initiated—with some progress evident—only to come to a halt because of action by the management above the top person in the target system. Organizations must stress the importance of linkage with higher management and implement effective action to accomplish this linkage. This problem often results from a failure to include higher management in diagnosis, planning, implementation and/or evaluation.

The failure of effective linkage may result partly from disagreement among members of the change-agent teams and partly from the way change-agents relate to higher management.

Even when meetings to effect such linkage take place, failure may result from any untested, implicit, and unshared expectations, such as the top person's expectations about what he or she is required to do, a lack of competence among the change-agents, or excessive concern by the change agent about job security.

2. Linkages within the target system with other persons, issues and/or parts: vertical and horizontal, line and staff.

Even when top management are included in the change program and they become more authentic and open with each other, these behavioral changes may not occur in the transactions between the top managers and their immediate or distant subordinates. Change programs may affect insulated parts of the client system and may not reach other organizational units or affect more than one or two dimensions of a given unit's operation. Thus, linkage with several levels of people within the target system may be a good element to be designed into a change program. Such linkage could take the form of working on operating problems, which involves units other than the original focal unit, or it could take the form of involving large numbers and many levels of system members at the problem-identification phase of the change program.

Differences among successful OD efforts

The issues mentioned above can be managed in many ways. There is no one best way, only ways which are more or less comfortable for—or familiar to—the change agents and which may or might not be effective.

At least three different types of *conceptual models* might be introduced by change-agents for diagnosis and to help system members to consider improvement goals regarding a dimension or operation central to the target system's effective performance—that is, how target-system members think they should try to operate their organization. Most OD programs, however, involve more than just one type.

Cognitive. The Blake and Mouton Managerial Grid workshop, for example, consists of assigned readings, tests, and demonstration exercises.

Process. This model focuses on how system members relate to each other—e.g., how they think the exercise of authority influenced their effectiveness.

Procedural. This model guides or coaches system members through a carefully controlled series of steps in identifying, diagnosing, and planning action regarding problems in the operation of the target system.

Variations exist in the manner in which models for formulating goals are introduced into the client system, which are then incorporated into the practices of the system, i.e., the models become institutionalized.

The change-agent presents formal training programs. The change-agent sets a behavioral example, describes intentions, and illustrates them. Procedures described and illustrated are then disseminated throughout the system.

*A review and synopsis of Paul Buchanan's examination of 10 cases of organizational development "Crucial Issues in Organizational Development" in *Change in School Systems*, Goodwin Watson, Ed., Washington, D.C.: NTL Institute for COPED, 1967.

The change-agent helps system members identify "spontaneously emerging solutions to problems" by "listening for the principles and concepts behind the words" and holding them up for examination and comparison with current practices through demonstration, using "self" as a model.

The change-agent demonstrates how various problem-solving procedures can be used.

Internal or external (outside) consultants function as managers of the OD program. The location of the change-agent does not seem to be in itself a crucial factor, but location may be related to the role of the change agent in planning, the change agent's motivations, who her or his "client" is, and her or his job security.

Most successful OD programs involve all levels of target-system management, but may differ in the time at which additional levels become involved. The change-agent may not be needed at all levels; when significant changes on a central issue are made at the top, they may spread throughout the subordinate organization.

Similarities among successful OD efforts

1. The top manager of the target system is actively involved in the project. This does not differentiate successful projects from unsuccessful ones. Determining the boundaries of the target system may be most vital, for this determines the top manager.

2. The change-agent introduces a viable model for collecting data and for diagnosing the system's needs which can be used by system members to establish goals for improvement.

3. Regardless of the model or when it is introduced into the system, the problem-solving processes of the system should focus upon it in an explicit manner.

4. OD projects tend to lead to changes in the power structure of the target system, i.e., changes in

- the kind of power or influence used (from authority to use of information);

- the distribution of influence (proportionately more influence by people at lower levels);

- the total amount of influence exerted (target-system members feel a sense of control over events rather than being subjects of external forces or chance).

5. Norms and standards of behavior and skills are developed which facilitate a shift away from relationships based on negotiations or bargaining toward those based on problem solving or collaboration.

6. The change-agent comes from outside the target system and is new to the target system, although he or she may originate from within the larger system of which the target is part. This does not, however, differentiate successful OD projects from unsuccessful ones.

Ten Characteristics Predictive of Successful Efforts at Organization Development

1. There is pressure from the environment, internal or external, for change.

2. Some strategic person or people are "hurting."

3. Some strategic people are willing to do a real diagnosis of the problems.

4. Leadership is provided by a line executive, key staff person, and/or consultant.

5. There is collaborative identification of problems between line and staff people.

6. There is some willingness to take risks in new relationships or new organization forms.

7. There is a realistic, long-term perspective.

8. There is a willingness to face the situation and to work on changing it.

9. The system rewards people for the effort of changing and improvement, not just for short-term results.

10. There are tangible, intermediate results.

Ten Conditions for Failure of Efforts at Organization Development

1. A continued discrepancy exists between top management's statements of values or styles and its actual managerial behavior; top managers say one thing and do another.

2. The organization has a large program of activities without any clear goals for change.

3. There is confusion between ends and means. The question of "training for what" must be answered.

4. There is a short-term perspective. A realistic time framework for organizational change is at least three to five years.

5. There is a lack of coordination among a number of different activities aimed at increasing organizational effectiveness.

6. There is an overdependence on others, either on outside consultants or inside specialists.

7. A large gap exists between commitment to change at the top of the organization and the transfer of this interest to the middle of the organization.

8. The organization tries to fit a major organizational change into an old organizational structure.

9. There is a constant search for cookbook solutions.

10. The organization applies an intervention or strategy inappropriately, or tends to apply someone else's package.

Evaluation of Consultative Services

Arthur M. Freedman

An evaluation might consist of a comparison between the previously stated and validated—by both consultants and client-system members—consultation objectives and the actual results of the consultation. This requires that the objectives be stated in observable, measurable, verifiable, behavioral terms. It also requires both consultants and client-system members to make the comparison in a self-conscious and explicit fashion at the conclusion of the consultation.

Example

Problem (felt and evident)

In their administrative meetings, members of the top-management group all say—without being specific—that they are in mutual agreement about the philosophy and objectives of their organization. During the diagnostic phase, however, when consultants asked each manager individually what these were, there was little actual agreement.

Objective (validated by all parties)

In an administrative meeting, all members of the top-management group explicitly specify their organization's philosophy and objectives to the extent that each member verbally acknowledges and states at least that he or she understands, accepts, and is willing to act in accord with both a written organizational philosophy and a list of two or more specific organizational objectives, One of these is a mid-range (six-year) objective.

Note that with an objective stated in this manner, evaluation might consist of a simple check: "Did this described event occur or not?"

Evaluation techniques

Donald L. Kirkpatrick (1975) describes four classes of "techniques for evaluating training programs" and illustrates them by examples. Basically, these classes are

1. **Reaction.** Client-system members'—or training program participants'—reactions to the consultation or training program: how they felt, what they thought. These kinds of data can be obtained through a more or less straightforward questionnaire.

2. **Learning.** What client-system members or training-program participants actually learned as a consequence of the consultation or training in terms of facts, concepts, and processes or procedures. These data might be obtained through oral or written "tests" and simulations or role plays.

3. **Behavior.** Whether or not client-system members or training-program participants actually applied what they learned through the consultation or training to their actual job setting. These data may be obtained through self- or peer report and direct observation of job performance or indirect (unobtrusive) measures.

4. **Results.** Whether or not the application of learnings derived from the consultation or training resulted in any real differences in the client-system members' behavior, work procedures, or organizational policies and structures. These data can be obtained through self- or peer reports, business records, and direct observation of on-the-job performance, or indirect observation.

In examining the reaction-learning-behavior-results levels of evaluation, it may be useful to also think about the implications of what Don Campbell and Don Fisk refer to as the "multi-source/multi-method" approach to research and evaluation.

Multi-source refers to the notion of not depending upon only one source of evaluative data. In the absence of at least a second and, if possible, a third source of data, one could find oneself relying upon a single—and biased—evaluative point of view. An example of multi-source would be the following:

a. self-report;
b. trainer's or consultant's impressions;
c. "objective" observer's perceptions; and
d. significant (back-home) others' perceptions and reactions.

Multi-method refers to the desirability of employing many different media or techniques of measuring results. These could include observation check lists, questionnaires, physiological tests (e.g., heart rate, blood pressure), open-ended or structured interviews, and the like. The general idea is to "triangulate" on a particular result without having to depend upon just one indicator of that result. Any one methodological indicator may be just as biased as any one source of evaluative information in the sense that a single method is likely to be "sensitive" to and, therefore, yield a measurement of some observable behaviors while being "insensitive" to other important dimensions.

Reference

Kirkpatrick, D. L. *Evaluating training programs*. Madison, WI: ASTD, 1975.

Client Feedback to Consultant

Barry Oshry

Consultant's Name _____

Your Name _____

What is your position and function within the system with which the consultant is working?

_____

_____

From your point of view, how did the consultant get involved with your system (your organization)?

_____

_____

Did you think that the consultant was pretty much the same kind of a person as you and your associates?
_____ yes _____ no   Please specify.

_____

_____

Did you think that in some way the consultant did not seem to fit in with you and your associates? That he or she was different somehow? _____ yes _____ no   Please specify.

_____

_____

Did you think that the consultant was sympathetic to your position or your condition? That he or she cared about you and your associates? _____ yes _____ no   Please specify.

_____

_____

Did you think the consultant was an important influence on the decisions which you and your associates had to make?
_____ yes _____ no   Please specify.

_____

_____

Did you think that the consultant was a person whom you and your associates could trust? _____ yes _____ no Please specify.

_____

_____

Did you think that the consultant was expressing his or her true feelings when consulting with you and your associates? _____ yes _____ no Please specify.

_____

_____

Did you think that you could depend upon the consultant to act in a consistent and predictable manner? _____ yes _____ no Please specify.

_____

_____

Did you think that the consultant's own personal desires or needs interfered with either the effectiveness or the appropriateness of the consultative work he or she contracted to do? _____ yes _____ no Please specify.

_____

_____

****

How would describe the relationship between the consultant and you and your associates? To what extent did you feel that...

...the way the consultant acted gave us the impression that he/she felt that our ideas weren't any good, that only the consultant's ideas were worth anything, and that we should do things the way he or she thought they should be done. When we did the things the consultant wanted in his/her way, things seemed alright.

| Very much | 6 | 5 | 4 | 3 | 2 | 1 | Not at all |

...the consultant seemed to ignore us when we tried to make suggestions or provide him or her with information. The consultant gave us the impression that he or she wanted to do everything alone, as if he or she didn't want to work with us or share the work.

| Very much | 6 | 5 | 4 | 3 | 2 | 1 | Not at all |

...the consultant tried to prevent us from doing the work we were supposed to do. The consultant seemed to feel that when we did our work the way we thought we should, this was an attack on him or her or a criticism of the kind of help he or she was trying to give us.

| Very much | 6 | 5 | 4 | 3 | 2 | 1 | Not at all |

...we (client system members) were able to depend upon each other. We seemed to be able to respect and to influence one another.

| Very much | 6 | 5 | 4 | 3 | 2 | 1 | Not at all |

Consultant Checklist:
For Use During Practice Consultations

BARRY OSHRY

Each of the following represents a condition of effective "consultation-helping-development" work. As you examine your role in this consultation *at this time*, to what extent is each "condition" true *for you*?

1 = Not at all
2 = Very little
3 = Somewhat
4 = Quite a bit
5 = A great deal

_____ 1. CLARITY   I think that I understand this client system very clearly. I understand its dynamics, structure, leadership patterns, norms, etc.

_____ 2. CONNECTEDNESS   I feel in touch with people in this client system. I feel that I know them and that they know me. I do not feel alienated or distant from them.

_____ 3. CARING   I care about people in this client system. I care about what happens to them.

_____ 4. RESOURCES   I think that I have resources—i.e., skills, abilities, techniques, ideas—which can be of assistance to this client system.

_____ 5. CONSULTING TEAM COHERENCE   I am working in synchrony with the other consultants; we are working together and not at cross purposes.

_____ 6. MARGINALITY   I am able to be both a part of this client system and apart from it. I am neither so far out as to lose my effectiveness, nor so far in that I lose my perspective and objectivity.

_____ 7. AUTHENTICITY   I talk straight with people in this client system; I don't have to be overly cautious or pussyfoot around.

_____ 8. USE OF POTENTIAL I am using what I've got to give to this client system. My most important skills, abilities, resources, and ideas are being used in this client system.

During practice consultations, or when consulting "for real," learning may be derived from stopping your work from time to time to reflect upon *what* you have been doing and *how* you have been doing all of "that." This checklist focuses on eight dimensions of the art and science of "consultancy," regardless of the specific style or role being performed. If you are working as part of a consulting team, there may be some value for each team member to rate themselves and each other along these dimensions, then share and discuss these ratings.

Managing Internal and External OD Consultants

Stanley R. Hinckley, Jr.

There are many ways in which one could talk wisely about how to manage internal and external consultants, but the important and key elements fall into categories: the terms of a good contract between the manager of OD and a consultant, and a collection of good advice for the manager. For the former category, the terms can be sorted into those which apply to both internal and external consultants, those which apply only to internal, and those which apply only to external. So, this paper is organized in the form of half of the dialogue which, I believe, should take place periodically between a manager of OD and each consultant who reports directly or indirectly to her/him. The advice for the manager is similarly presented in the form of half the internal dialogue which a person in such a role needs to have going on almost continuously.

Messages to both internal and external consultants

1. You must take the major portion of the responsibility for building your own reputation as a good consultant. I will provide to your clients, and to potential clients, honest recommendations for you—and I will tell you what I tell them—but I will not tell them about the areas in which you need more experience, unless (a) I think the client can use that information well and (b) you and I agree beforehand that it would be useful to do so.

2. I expect you to do careful and ongoing diagnoses of the client systems, using me and other internal resources to assist you.

3. I expect you to use me as a consultant to you in developing strategies and action plans.

4. I expect your behavior to be consistent at all times with the values and concepts which you are working to have adopted and implemented in your client systems.

5. I expect you to be continually assessing your own strengths and needs for greater knowledge and skills.

You hold the primary responsibility for obtaining good feedback from me and from others, to corroborate your self-assessment.

6. I expect you to spend effort and energy on developing new technology, that is, to invent and test new interventions and to develop new concepts which work.

7. The most important criteria I will use in evaluating your performance are:

(a) the nature and the extent of the positive changes that occur in your client systems because of your efforts;

(b) the quality of the definition of the change projects developed by you and your clients;

(c) your ability to "move up" in your client systems—that is, to develop consulting relationships with managers closer and closer to the top of the system and to work on system issues and problems which are closer and closer to the "heart" of the organization's work and its dynamics;

(d) your success in generating your own clients;

(e) your ability to use any client's discomfort with your work as a learning opportunity for all; and

(f) the accuracy of your self-assessments.

8. I will provide you with *all* the information I receive about what is happening in our organization and in its environment; some of this information will be confidential—something I am not supposed to share with you. When this happens, I will tell you and expect you not to share the information with anyone. We will discuss how the information affects your work and how it cannot be used. If it appears to me that the information I am giving you is creating more ambiguity and uncertainty than you are comfortable with, I will consult with you about how to cope better with the situation.

9. Sometimes I will translate information I receive into a form which I believe will be helpful or, at least, neutral in

its impact on you and your work. If you hear something different from another source and see a discrepancy between what I told you and what you've heard elsewhere, I expect you to check out that discrepancy with me.

10. I will share all feedback I receive on your work with you. I know that some of the feedback will be "flaky" because of a client's inability sometimes to understand what you're doing, or because of clients' need to protect themselves from facing some aspects of their situations. I will do my best to help us both interpret the feedback in useful ways, to decide whether and how to respond to it, and to determine how it affects your strategies and behavior, and mine.

11. I will do my best to prevent the organization from developing a stereotype of you and your capabilities. We do not want them to see you as "only good at X" or as "an advocate for Y." At the same time, you may be a specialist in certain areas, which I will support while encouraging you to broaden your expertise.

12. You will probably need to have a "bags packed" attitude much of the time, meaning that you will be developing viable options for yourself continually, both in terms of potential clients and projects within the organization and in terms of possible alternative career or employment options.

13. I want you to teach me and other consultants what you know and what you are learning, and I want opportunities to do the same with you.

14. My decisions and recommendations about assignments and projects for you will be based on my initial assessment of the scope of the potential work and its likely direction, and on my assessment of your capabilities and interests. You have the right to know and understand the basis for my decisions and to obtain my involvement in working out any disagreements between us.

The issues and dilemmas inherent in a marginal role such as internal or external OD consultant, and in the role of the manager of OD, are probably clear enough in the above messages that further explanation is not needed. I do want to emphasize the importance for any consultant of the "bags packed" attitude. Having viable and known options available provides the independence and self-confidence often needed to stand up against any client system's efforts to generate collusion with maintaining the status quo. There are times when acceptance of the status quo, or of the client's slower timetable for change, is strategically smart, but these choices need to be made cleanly and without pressure from oneself or from others to maintain the contract. Refusing to continue to work with a system or an

individual is sometimes the best intervention that one can make, especially if the reasons for the decision are fully explained to the client. For external consultants, dependence on any one organization for more than one-third of one's business is not wise, although there may be periods of a few months when more work with that organization meets their needs and yours.

Additional messages to internal consultants

15. I expect you to be able at any time to articulate your recent accomplishments and your needs for professional development. I expect you to spend up to 10% of your time each year on your own development, and I will provide approval of the time and money required, limited only by our mutual judgment of the relevance of your plans to both organizational needs and your own needs, and by any organizational constraints which, after hard testing, I am not able to change.

16. Evaluation of your performance will be based on data you and I obtain from your clients, your colleagues, and from my own assessment. I expect to have the majority vote on the decisions made by this organization regarding your salary, your title, and your assignments. I will "work the system" to the best of my ability to obtain decisions which are based on your proven capabilities and your potential, and which are fair and consistent with the internal and external markets for your skills and knowledge.

17. I will help you build a reputation outside of this organization by introducing you to those outside people and organizations with which I have connections, and by providing honest recommendations to them. Occasionally, I may be able to arrange outside work for you, but you must do most of the work required to become known by others, to find opportunities for outside work, to make presentations at conferences, and to publish.

A special message to external consultants

18. I expect and need you to act sometimes as if I were your only client and at other times to act as if you were my manager. In the latter case, I want you to be tracking me and helping me in all of the areas described above, and I will do the same for you.

There is one additional issue which a manager and all consultants struggle with frequently. In my experience, most clients want the "best consultant in the world" to work on their projects. Since few of them know how to assess a consultant's capabilities in this strange technology called "OD," they rely on credentials and reputations excessively. Recommending a consultant, internal or external, to a manager is fraught with pitfalls. If the recommendation is not glowing and doesn't indicate that the consultant can do everything except miracles, the client may feel that he or she is getting second-or-third-best. This exacerbates any discomfort they may already experience with the power the manager of OD has to decide which consultant to have. If the recommendation is so positive that it hides some important information about the consultant's real skills and experience, any subsequent difficulties with the work will come as an unfortunate surprise to the client. The reaction then is likely to be one of "Why didn't you tell me so I could have supervised the project more carefully?" On the other hand, an accurate description of a proposed consultant's strengths and weaknesses often leads to a reduction in the client's willingness to trust what the consultant does and says, in some cases dooming the work to failure. I have no solutions to this dilemma, other than to emphasize the importance of identifying and discussing with the client any assumptions he or she seems to be making about what the consultant can or cannot do. Of course, the ultimate solution is to educate all managers in how to manage change and in how to manage and utilize consultants well.

Messages to yourself, the manager of OD

1. Be clear with yourself about when you are being a manager and when you are being a consultant. When in doubt, be the manager, because if you don't, there's no one else to do it, and there are always other consultants around ready to show what they can do.

2. Convert as much of the work being done as possible to projects with clear objectives and rough schedules.

3. Watch for patterns in your own thinking and behavior that indicate that you are being influenced by your own unconscious assumptions about people who differ in race, gender, educational level, or socio-economic background.

4. Get the right consultant involved as early as possible, avoiding the temptation to be the consultant to the manager with a potential project until the work is clearly defined. The two of you may define the work so that it fits your own values and skills more than those of the person who will be doing most of the work.

5. Test all the consultant's plans against the goal of making the organization a more effective human system, and be clear and articulate about the connection between that goal and all work.

6. Watch the values, norms, and procedures being followed and developed in your unit, and make sure that they're consistent with those you're advocating to clients.

7. Matching the right consultant with the right work is extremely important, and also difficult. Involving the client and consultants in the decision-making process is usually better than not, but it requires that you be clear about all the important factors to be considered.

8. Be extremely sensitive to the degree of respect and trust you have from the top of the organization. Your ability to manage the function and to obtain high-quality work from the consultants depends on your power to assure that evaluations of the work being done and of the people who are doing it are fair.

9. Make your first priority the education of clients in how to use and manage consultants well and in how to develop and define good change projects. Help them to appreciate that they are an important part of the system that needs changing and cannot remain aloof from any project in their organization.

10. Make your second priority the coaching, counseling and teaching of internal consultants. Provide them with the resources and support they need to develop professionally and avoid the trap of trying to be their guru.

11. Organize work so that it requires two or more consultants whenever possible. Most work does not justify more than one person, and many consultants prefer the autonomy of working alone, and so even marginal opportunities to pair consultants should be used.

12. A critical skill for you is getting good feedback from clients and from your own observations and transforming the data into clear and useful information for the internal and external consultants.

13. Recognize that all feedback on the consultants is also feedback for you. It may often say more about how you're managing than about anyone else's performance.

14. Insist that all feedback be given directly to the person whose behavior evoked it. When the giver refuses to give it directly, try for a three-party meeting. If that won't work, make sure you complete the loop back to the giver, telling him or her the outcomes of your use of the information.

15. Don't accept any feedback from anyone without responding immediately. It is essential to get clear about the giver's purpose in telling you and what he or she expects you to do with the information. It is also essential to determine the extent to which negative feedback is being communicated to protect the giver from some discomfort that you should not allay. An immediate response, informing the giver of your evaluation of the feedback and advising her or him of what you will and will not do with it, will avoid many problems later.

16. Prevent clients and consultants from engaging in non-specific comparisons of consultants to each other, including yourself, no matter how much such discussion might do for your own ego or someone else's.

17. Watch out for using yourself as the yardstick against which you judge all other consultants. This requires a very accurate self-assessment and an unbiased view of the wide range of knowledge, skills, styles, and approaches that are effective with different clients on different kinds of work.

18. If you must have your own consulting work to be happy, choose projects which are as separate as possible from those that other internal and external consultants are working on, or pair up with one of them. Do not choose work for yourself which is consistently more visible, or prestigious, or important in the organization.

19. Don't try to hold conventional team-building sessions with your group of internal consultants and staff. Their tendency (and yours!) to be competitive with each other can lead to no participants in the session, just consultants. Do hold group meetings periodically on the mission of the function, the overall strategy for change, and the structure of the function to do the work. Also use group meetings for educational purposes and for cross-training, including external consultants as much as possible. In periods of high stress, group meetings focused on strategies or on evaluating progress will provide adequate opportunities for venting and for mutual support.

20. Watch the stress levels on the consultants and on the client systems, and use the data to open up discussions with the appropriate consultants about the diagnosis, the strategy, and the tactics.

21. Refuse all work clearly aimed at "fixing" a part of the organization or an individual. Managers rarely appreciate the extent to which the environment of an individual or group determines their performance. Therefore, they overlook their own part of the problem. It is better to ignore an individual or group than to try to fix them. It is best to redefine the problem into one that lies between the system and the individual or group rather than act on a problem that is located within them.

22. Be clear about the criteria you are using in selecting external consultants. The more important ones are

— intelligence and competence;

— ability to develop good change projects and make them happen;

— knowledge and skills in an area in which the internal staff needs to develop;

— ability to work with internal consultants as colleagues;

— ability to be open with you and your staff, especially about your behavior and their own;

— ability and willingness to train others;

— acceptance of management's ultimate responsibility for the business and the organization.

23. The same criteria are good for hiring experienced internal consultants. The ratio of learners to experienced people on an internal staff needs to be planned carefully and should never exceed 2:1, but of course, there are not just two categories. The most important determinant of staff competence is the nature of the work and management's skill level in managing change.

24. Keep the ratio of external to internal consultants working in the organization between 70:30 and 25:75. In most cases, the optimum is probably closer to the 25:75 ratio for reasons of cost and, more importantly, to provide the on-site availability, follow-up, and schedule flexibility needed for a successful change effort.

Obviously, this half of the dialogue is for a manager of OD who is also a consultant. I do not think it is possible to be good at managing OD consultants without also having pretty good consulting skills oneself. An in-depth knowledge of OD is not essential if the person has considerable experience in managing, especially in the same organization. In this context, line-management experience is much more valuable than staff-management experience. No one can manage an OD function without understanding the technology and the business of the organization.

The applicability of the material in this paper to anyone's particular situation must be determined by that person. The process of developing a set of messages which do apply to the individual's situation is highly recommended since it requires articulating one's knowledge and experience and forces a good diagnosis of both the organizational setting and one's own capabilities, interests, and vision.

Similarities and Differences of Internal and External Consultants

Donald H. Swartz

Definitions

The Internal Consultant is a helper—professional or nonprofessional—who is considered a member of the client system or a closely related system.

The External Consultant is a helper—usually professional—who has minimal or no organizational/political relationship with the client system.

Why this subject?

Why might a discussion of similarities and differences between internal and external consulting situations be important? I see three answers to this question:

1. A consultant's effectiveness depends primarily on his or her professional behavior. An internal consultant may behave quite differently from an external consultant—even when working in the same consulting situation. For example, the internal consultant may exercise extreme caution because he or she "has to live with the client." The external person has the option to leave and thus can behave in a more objective, aggressive manner.

2. Consulting behavior can be adjusted appropriately if the consultant is aware of the situational differences (and the major reasons for those differences) between internal and external types.

3. The experience of professional consultants tells us that the most effective consultation occurs when external and internal consultants "team consult." In these situations, awareness of similarities and differences is critical in order to match "flat sides"—that is, to complement each other's strengths and limitations.

Role similarities

Whether external or internal, consulting roles are similar in these ways:

1. Both are helpers.

2. They must get their job done through others who don't report to them organizationally. They do not have "power" by virtue of legitimate authority as line managers.

3. They work with and through client-system members using forms of influence other than formal authority.

4. They can be called in by the client or imposed upon the client by forces outside the client system.

5. They can both play multiple consulting roles.

6. They both want to be successful.

Situational differences

The differences between internal and external consultant types result from the unique situations each must confront. Outlined below are some of these situational differences.

Internal Consultant

1. As part of the system, usually knows the language and background of the problem.

2. As part of the system, may be a part of the problem.

3. Usually will give more time to the client because of availability and costs.

4. Sometimes encounters resistance because of vested interests and organizational politics.

5. Subsystem tends to seem as if things are "o.k."

6. Usually knows the norms and political realities better than someone from outside.

7. An internal consultant is not seen as a "prophet" in her or his own organization.

8. Internal consultant knows more about potential "linkage" with other parts of system.

*MCB Publications Limited, Bradford, U.K. *Journal of European Industrial Training*, Vol. 4, No. 5, 1975. Used by permission.

9. Usually identifies with the system's needs/pains/aspirations.

10. A "known" quantity.

11. May lack perspective.

12. May not have required special knowledge or skill.

13. May have to live down past failure or affiliations.

External Consultant

1. Usually has more "influence" with client system. Seen as "expert" (prophet).

2. Usually has more varied experiences; broader perspective.

3. Usually more objective about the client and the problem; independent of the client power structure.

4. Pay and continued use are usually tied to results.

5. Is usually aware of other resources that might be helpful to the client.

6. Client tends to be more open with the external consultant about needing help.

7. Free to leave the situation when consultation is complete.

8. Client usually has high expectations that may verge on inappropriate dependency.

9. Free to reject the consulting assignment.

10. In a position to introduce "new" things into the client system.

Some suggested behavior and actions

For the internal consultant

1. *Behave like an external consultant.* This requires careful role clarification between consultant and client. In addition, a strong psychological contract characterized by mutual trust and openness is a must before entering any consulting relationship.

2. *Do some outside (external) consulting.* Whether for pay or free, external experience can broaden perspective, increase internal credibility, and increase consultant confidence. Outside experience provides an arena for experimentation. In some instances, it can provide a significant part of the financial security required to support the internal consultant when he or she finds it

appropriate to confront or be brutally objective with the internal client system.

3. *Be proactive and aggressive at least 25% of the time.* It's important for the internal consultant to introduce change ideas as well as to help clients to respond to unplanned change. Influence power accrues to the consistent, responsible innovator.

4. *Focus on the job to be done.* The internal consultant survives and grows in direct proportion to the client's effectiveness in getting the job done. All consulting activities—even awareness-experience labs—must be focused on the job to be done. There is a saying that applies to internal consultants: "If you put the turkey on the table, you won't have to eat crow."

5. *Be your own person.* No one owns you. No one manipulates you. No one can change you any more than you can change them.

For the external consultant

1. *Don't take on an assignment if your gut says "no."* Feelings about the client and client-system norms/values/methods should be allowed to surface. This means precontract data gathering and some face-to-face meetings with the client. Then, trust your feelings.

2. *Study the client system; learn the language.* Empathy for the client system is critical to building trust. Empathy is best achieved when the consultant understands and appreciates the culture of the client system. The external consultant may get along famously with the client, but fail to get close to the system if he or she "can't speak the language."

3. *Don't bypass internal helpers.* Involve internal helpers (personnel, OD, training) as early as possible in contracts with the client. Encourage the client to keep them "clued in." External consultants are a natural threat to internal helpers. Without their (internal helpers') understanding and, at the very least, their neutrality, the external consultant's work could be subtly sabotaged.

4. *Work collaboratively with internal consultants.* If a qualified internal helper is not apparent, encourage the client to find one. A collaborative working relationship between internal and external consultants is valuable. It is a powerful approach and, I am convinced, a necessary one if the positive changes sought through consultative intervention are to be gained and sustained.

5. *Leave the inside consultant with increased power.* A major contribution that external consultants make to client systems is helping them to gain strength to cope with their problems without outside help. A skilled internal consultant in a legitimate helper role is essential to the client system's ability to self-renew. The external consultant should be constantly helping her or his internal counterpart gain credibility in the organization.

6. *Be human.* External consultants are expected to be pros; they're not expected to be gods. The external consultant who takes the calculated risk, who occasionally leaves the comfort of a "proven technique" to respond

more effectively to unique client-system needs, who can say forthrightly, "I goofed! Now what can we learn from that?" is the person I want to work with. Freedom to fail is the target. Fear of failure is the block.

Strategy Guidelines for an Internal Organization Development Unit*

Roger Harrison

These guidelines are intended as a checklist or reminder, rather than as a comprehensive treatise on organization development (OD) strategy. My concern here is only with strategy, and not with the goals the strategy is intended to achieve. These notes are relevant to OD means, not ends. I expect many of the points will be self-evident to experienced OD practitioners and hope that they all provoke thought and planning on the part of others.

Major strategic problems of an internal OD unit

1. To gain influence based on expertise and ability to help, rather than influence through channels of authority and power. To deploy limited economic and human resources in ways that maximize impact.

2. To develop the skills and knowledge of the internal agents of change in the organization.

3. To maintain the OD unit and to preserve the group and its members against the detrimental effects of pressure and stress. In so doing, to remain independent of organizational pressures for conformity of thought and action while maintaining confidence and trust on the part of organization members.

Guidelines for gaining appropriate influence and deploying resources effectively

1. Work with the forces in the organization that are supportive of change and improvement, rather than work against those who are defensive and resistant. It is better to find someone who wants to help and to work with that person than it is to try and convince a skeptic of the need for OD assistance. Wherever possible, follow the path of least organizational resistance to OD goals rather than confronting resistance. This implies not doing anything across the board: no mass training, no wholesale installa-

*Reprinted from *OD Practitioner*, 1972, Vol. 4, No. 3. Used by permission of Harrison Kouzes Associates.

tion of Management By Objectives, no involvement of the entire organization in staff development programs. The limited OD resources available are weakened and absorbed by the organization in such frontal assaults on problems, and the results are invariably disappointing.

2. Try to develop "critical mass" in each change project, a self-sustaining organization-improvement process that is motivated and powered from within the system that is changing. To do this, resources available to the OD unit must be concentrated on the target system for a time, to get the process underway. Organizations are self-stabilizing systems which can absorb a great deal of energy from the outside without changing very much. Investments of resources that are insufficient to move the system beyond its natural equilibrium are wasteful and unproductive.

3. When working with a given system, try to find multiple entry points into it: a variety of people, groups, processes, and problems with which contact can be made and to which help may be given. It is useful when approaching a particular organization or subsystem to brainstorm all the possible points of contact which might be used and all the different ways in which the unit could offer useful help to the system. As many of these multiple entries as feasible can then be attempted.

4. Look for "felt needs," problems recognized by managers which can be dealt with by OD techniques and processes. The best opportunities occur when you face problems for which there is no "standard" procedural or bureaucratic solution, and when the managers involved are really bothered by their difficulty in coping. Look for these problems when new technology is being introduced (e.g., computers); when a problem requires close collaboration and coordination across functional lines (e.g., mergers and takeovers); when organization restructuring of any kind is taking place; when physical locations are being changed or new plants and facilities being built and commissioned; or when the organization is expanding or contracting rapidly (e.g., redundancies).

5. Whenever possible, work with relatively healthy parts of the organization which have the will and the resources to improve. Avoid being seduced or pressured into working on "lost causes"—individuals or groups who have lost the ability to cope with the situation as it is. Usually change requires additional energy and talent during the period of transition. Performance initially

worsens even after the most beneficial changes until people learn how to make the changed organization work up to its potential. Persons or groups whose performance is substandard or barely adequate usually cannot afford and are not allowed the additional resources and period of further decreased performance which is required to change successfully. They are often unusually defensive in their reaction to outsiders offering "help."

Unfortunately, higher management may put great pressure on an OD unit to work with the more ineffective subsystems, sometimes on the assumption that the offending group is so far gone anyway that little harm can be done even by an incompetent intervention.

6. Work with individuals and groups which have as much freedom and discretion in managing their own operations as possible. It profits nothing to work out an agreed change with a manager who turns out not to have the latitude to carry it out. It is equally useless to work on a change with someone who feels dominated and controlled from above and who therefore cannot muster the courage to risk experimenting on her or his own. These considerations cast great doubt on the wisdom of management training and staff development programs for lower levels of staff and supervisors unless the programs actively involve the management levels where effective control resides.

7. Try to obtain appropriate and realistic levels of involvement in the program of the OD unit on the part of top management. This does not mean that the highest levels of management must necessarily be "at the cutting edge of change." They are too often too personally identified with the status quo for this to be possible. Except in times of emergency, the system tends to stabilize itself by placing people in the top positions whose values and styles perpetuate the accepted ways of doing things. Often the best supporters of an OD unit are among the ranks of management just below the top where the personal commitment to the present is less, and where the drive for achievement and advancement may be higher than at the very top.

There are three levels of commitment to OD objectives from top management which can be helpful. The minimum is giving permission for change to occur. Top management sees the necessity of change, at least at an intellectual level, and allows it to occur without active opposition. The unspoken qualifier is usually "as long as *we* don't have to do anything different."

The next level is that of support and encouragement for change. The involvement in change activities of other parts of the organization is facilitated, and higher management monitors and evaluates the changes achieved. As before, however, the actual changes in work and relationship patterns do not extend to the highest levels. The latter are insulated from actual change.

The third level is participation in change, in which the higher management actively involves itself in the change process, often as a client for OD assistance. While this level is the most satisfactory, it is rarely achieved in practice. The failure to involve top management actively in the change process sets an upper limit on what can be accomplished, but the other levels of commitments will permit considerable useful work to be done. Unfortunately, in many change programs, it is not clear that even the first level, permission, has been achieved, and such programs are usually rather ineffective.

8. Try to establish direct communication and contact with all levels of the organization. Try to develop customs and accepted practices of operating which exempt OD-unit members from following normal bureaucratic channels or the "chain of command." OD practitioners cannot work effectively through formal authority or by using sources of coercive power. The only way they can influence anyone is through expertise, persuasion, and helpfulness. Direct contact and discussion with clients and with sources of information and support are vital, and reliance on intermediaries, no matter how well intentioned, hampers the work badly.

9. Develop confidence and credibility on the part of organization members through situations where the OD unit's unique expertise shows to best advantage. One good way for behaviorally oriented OD practitioners to develop trust and confidence on the part of potential clients is in the course of experiential, action-oriented training programs. In the atmosphere of openness and confrontation which often develops in each program, the client has a chance to size up the practitioner's ability to handle difficult situations effectively. Not only educational situations are a good way of allowing the client some low-risk opportunities to evaluate the contribution of the practitioner, but also diagnostic studies present chances to begin discussion with a client. Many projects begin with a commitment to joint study of a problem that commits neither client nor practitioner to go further.

10. Don't be afraid to ask to become involved in activities in which you think you may be able to make a contribution. Go directly to the potential client and tell her or him what you may be able to do to help. Since the client probably does not know much about what you have to offer, the person is unlikely to think of coming to the OD unit for help. The worst the client can do is say no. Proactive practitioners get many more opportunities to contribute than do passive ones.

11. Make known what the OD unit is doing, particularly when you have successes to report—but only with the client's permission, of course. A major failing of OD units is in not reporting widely enough their activities and achievements. The modesty may be commendable, but it does not advance the task to let the activities remain unknown. One good way is to hold a seminar for interested parties in which the client and the practitioner make a joint presentation of the change project, preferably with an honest description of the difficulties and drawbacks, as well as the successes.

12. Use outside consultants in ways that enhance—rather than compete with—the credibility of OD-unit members. For example, outsiders are often used to

develop entry to top management because OD-unit members do not have high enough organizational status to be acceptable as consultants at that level. If at all possible, the outsider should pair up with someone from the unit who works as closely with her or him as the client will permit.

Similarly, when outsiders are asked in to give courses and seminars, they should be paired with OD-unit members as co-trainers. A clear understanding should be developed that the two will work in such a way as to permit increased visibility for the inside person's skills and talents, as well as to enable the insider to learn what the outside consultant can teach.

Outsiders can sometimes also be used to gain acceptance for projects and to get them started. By involving the inside people from the beginning as co-workers, the latter can take over once the project is off the ground and run it with only occasional assistance from outside.

13. Link together people who are working to improve organization functioning, so their activities reinforce and complement one another. People working in such areas as training, methods improvement, computer technology, and human-resource planning are all working in areas related to organization development. Frequently they are in different functional lines and plan and conduct their work quite independently.

This splitting of resources reduces the likelihood of developing the "critical mass" referred to above, that self-sustaining change process which is the criterion of a really successful project. I feel strongly enough about the resulting wastage of resources to advocate the combining of these activities, either functionally or (perhaps as well) through some kind of matrix organization structure similar to the concept of the "business area." At the least, there should be some policy commitment supported by appropriate structure to ensure joint planning and coordination of strategy and projects, so that the organization-improvement activities would all support one another.

One example of such coordination is the linking of training (especially in such attitudinal/style areas as management, leadership, and effective group working) to follow up activities in the work situation. Any such training should be built into some on-the-job change activity of the OD practitioner (e.g., helping with problems of entry, diagnosis, team development, staff development). Attitudinal training and training in management style on an across-the-board basis should be avoided as a wasteful use of resources.

Training and OD activities can also be linked into technological, procedural, and structural changes stemming from application of management sciences to problems of rationalizing work. Such changes can be much more effectively implemented if there is adequate diagnosis of the readiness for and resistance to change, proper training of personnel who will be involved, and the establishment of ways of monitoring and dealing with

human problems that develop during the change process. Activities that lend themselves to this sort of joint approach are the introduction of computer technology, the implementation of mergers, takeovers and reorganizations, the starting up of new facilities, and the changing of work methods and procedures.

Guidelines for developing the skills and knowledge of internal change agents

1. A substantial proportion of the time of internal OD practitioners should be budgeted for their training and professional development. If they tend not to be professionally trained and to be relatively inexperienced, this should probably be about 20-25% of their time. Most of this training should be practical and experiential. Some useful training and development activities are the following:

• Pairing less experienced people with more experienced ones or with outside consultants on projects. The more experienced person advises and supports, but the less experienced one does the actual work on the project.

• Presentations and demonstrations of new techniques and processes by outsiders.

• Participation in some projects outside the company in which the practitioner takes the role of an external change-agent. These are more valuable, in my experience, for providing opportunities for taking increased responsibility and freedom to take reasonable risks—a freedom which may be prevented at home by the exposed situation of the OD unit. Dramatic increases in confidence and competence can be achieved by the judicious use of such outside experiences.

• Attendance at professional meetings and outside courses is also valuable, but I think less so than the other learning activities mentioned above.

2. Acquire a library of books and journals on OD and behavioral science applications. Make a special effort to retrieve techniques and instruments which have come into the hands of OD-unit members through their work with outside consultants or by their own invention. Keep an up-to-date list of who has had experience with what different approaches and methods, so that personnel know where to go for practical help.

3. Arrange learning activities between the related areas of training, management science, and behavioral applications. In the process of teaching others, people will become more competent in their own fields, and the cross-functional education will make it easier to work effectively together.

Guidelines for protecting OD practitioners from undue pressure and stress

1. Arrange most of the work in teams and pairs, for mutual learning and mutual support. People should not have to work alone in high-stress and high-risk situations until they are quite experienced.

2. Protect against premature evaluation of OD activities. Absorb a large proportion of the pressures from above and outside the unit in the senior manager(s) who are responsible. Management style in an OD unit should provide support and resources rather than direction, control, and evaluation. The clients may be depended upon for more than enough of the latter.

3. Make special pains to build strong, personal support relationships among OD-unit members. Frequent team-building sessions and some T Group or group-process work are helpful in achieving this. The use of an outside consultant to help build supportive internal relationships is frequently found helpful.

4. Develop career paths within and through the OD unit. The policy and practice should make it desirable for some to develop professional careers in change facilitation and for others to advance their line or staff careers by doing well in shorter (two- to three-year) assignments in the OD unit.

One way of using this checklist might be to review the current organization of OD activities in the light of the guidelines. I do not imagine that where the guidelines differ from current practice and policy it means the latter must be corrected; however, it may be that such discrepancies point to fruitful areas for discussion and decision.

Another way to use the guidelines is in planning particular change and development projects. The points can remind one of problems to be anticipated or resources which will be needed for a successful conclusion.

Similarly, it may help to review these ideas when faced with a particularly difficult problem in a project, or when an activity seems to go along poorly for no obvious reason. The framework provided may simply help to gain some perspective on the problem. Additionally, it may suggest diagnostic leads to the trouble or approaches to a solution.

Notes on the Marginality of the Consultant's Role

Newton Margulies

I am impressed with Ornstein's (1972) notion of the two sides of a person—the **rational** and the **intuitive**. The rational emphasizes the analytical, verbal, problem-solving, linear-thinking side that is reflected in much of our scientific and industrial development and, indeed, in the learning processes encouraged in our educational institutions. The other more intuitive side emphasizes the nonverbal, emotional, more esoteric, and even mystical approaches to learning, knowing, and being. There is a growing awareness that each person has both major modes of consciousness available: one rational, analytical, and linear, and the other arational, emotional, and intuitive. There also is a stream of thought which is attempting to achieve balance in these two different but complementary modes.

While the literature in organizational behavior abounds with pleas for integration, connection, and mutual development, theoretical models about a variety of behavioral phenomena (e.g., leadership, managing, communicating) still reflect the co-existence and maintenance of the poles as they are. Consultative models are also often discussed in terms of the polarity suggested by Ornstein.

Two consulting models

From one perspective, organizational consulting seems to have developed along two primary traditions. The first may be characterized as an approach that has as its major objective to provide a technical service to the client system. In the technical consulting model, the consultant is primarily concerned with bringing expertise to bear on a problem experienced by the client, and in this regard the consultant provides a service which the client does not have available. The relationship with the client is viewed as incidental to the problem-solving process, and generally the client is left to formulate a plan for the implementation of the proposed solutions.

The second approach regards consultation as a process which aims to facilitate an organizational diagnosis of the internal and sometimes external processes which affect the organization's behavior and subsequent performance.

This latter approach, commonly referred to as process consultation, is closely linked to the field of organizational development and is viewed as the central consulting mode employed by the OD practitioner.

Most would agree that the key behavioral characteristics of process consultation lie in the ability of the consultant to create an empathetic and symbiotic relationship with the client. In fact, to some extent, the effectiveness and satisfaction with the consulting projects undertaken is often attributed to the degree to which such a working relationship has been developed between client and consultant. Briefly, the best client-consultant relationship in this vein might be described as one in which there is considerable openness between client and consultant, mutuality of interest, shared responsibility for direction and outcomes of consulting projects, and ongoing feedback from one to another about behaviors relevant to the consulting project.

What I would like to suggest is that the role of the consultant is much more tenuous, much more marginal, and much more peripheral than is suggested by the process model and is nowhere as distant, uninvolved, and task-oriented as suggested by the technical model.

Staying on the fringe

Conceptually, the notion of marginality is not unlike what some social scientists have referred to as a **boundary position**. A boundary position is one in which the person is related to one particular work unit but belongs to another unit within the same organization, or belongs to another organization entirely. That is, the focal person does not belong to the social system with which he or she is working. The relevance of the boundary position is identified by the amount of time the boundary person spends with the unit as well as the importance attributed to the contact between the boundary person and the organizational units. Boundary positions, in general, tend to generate considerable personal stress, tension, and personal conflict. For consultants, this phenomenon is of particular interest since the personal strategies for resolving the stress and tension can, I hypothesize, have a major impact on the effectiveness of the consultant role.

My thesis is that effective consultation is related to the consultant's ability to build marginal relationships and to stay on the fringe, if you will, rather than to the consultant's ability to build close, sensitive, empathetic relationships with clients or to the consultant's ability to utilize his or her technical expertise. There are, then, a number of dimensions to the marginality of the consultant's role, several of which I will discuss here. The behavioral dilemma for the consultant is to first find the fringe area for each of these several dimensions and then to maintain the boundary relationship with the client rather than to assume any extreme or polar position. Several dilemmas will be touched on to illustrate the point.

Personal dilemmas

In terms of the two primary traditions of consulting in organizations, both the process and the technical consultation models seem to ignore the boundary notion and seem to work toward resolution of the personal dilemmas of the boundary position by identifying and suggesting the extreme behaviors for the consultant. Neither model seems to reflect the kind of consulting behavior which would necessarily lead to consultant effectiveness.

The involvement dilemma

The technical model implies that the consultant simply takes the client's statement of the problem at face value and provides the client with a technical solution. There is little need or emphasis in this model for building client-consultant relationships; there is little joint effort, and the consultant simply provides the best technical solution to the problem facing the client. In this model the consultant retains a detached, uninvolved stance and is interested only in an elegant solution to the problem. In the process model, on the other hand, the consultant works toward building an effective working relationship with the client characterized by open, confronting, involved behavior in which both client and consultant mutually work toward problem solving and organizational growth.

Each model, however, represents a polarized view of reality. The dangers are evident. In the technical model the consultant can become so detached from the client system that the necessary sensitivity to the client is affected. Whether or not the client system can muster resources to solve identified problems, and whether or not the consultant is indeed working on the "right" problems, may not be addressed.

In the process model, on the other hand, the consultant may be overly responsive to the client, and may become more a part of the client system than not. The usefulness of the consultant may diminish as the consultant becomes enmeshed in the organization. Further, should the consultant be seen and act more the advocate than the consultant, the role is additionally diminished. What

neither of these models indicates is the importance of a marginal role in which the consultant has the difficult job of maintaining the boundary position: being neither attached nor a part of the system but rather on the fine line between "being in and out."

The responsibility dilemma

In the technical consulting model, the consultant develops a strategy to resolve the client's problem. The consultant generally leaves the implementation of such solutions to the client. The process model stresses the importance of joint action between the client and consultant; a good deal of attention, however, is devoted to creating client ownership of the change process as well as of the implementation phase of problem solutions. Once again, it seems that each model provides an extreme view of the consultant's behavior in relation to the ownership of problems and problem solutions. In the boundary position the consultant neither owns nor disowns the process and the project; certain steps and phases reside with the consultant and the consultant assumes responsibility for these aspects. In other phases, the consultant insists that the client bear the major responsibility. In the boundary position the issue of ownership is not resolved through the medium of the consultant model or philosophy but is addressed selectively as the need arises. Ownership of the project is not something the consultant strives to put in the hands of the client, but is rather something to be examined and decided upon in light of the particular steps, phases, or activities that have to be accomplished.

The issue of responsibility is reflected in the concerns of many consultants. To what degree should I be responsible for specific change activities, and further, to what degree am I responsible for change in this client system? Again, the behavior of the consultant usually indicates that the dilemma is resolved in terms of either "the client is responsible" or "I am responsible," i.e., in one direction or the other. The effective response is probably on the fringe—there are aspects of responsibility that fall into the client's realm and those that fall into the consultant's. The conflict is at the boundary and cannot be easily resolved by relying on the extremes. Each situation must be faced at the boundary and resolved.

The acceptance dilemma

The difficulty for the consultant in the boundary role is to face the personal acceptance issue. For most consultants, the consulting role can be a lonely one, especially if the consultant intuitively functions on the boundary, being neither in nor out. The resolution of the acceptance issue then can be in terms of working toward acceptance by the client system or by electing to assume a consultation stance in which the issue does not have to be faced—that is, to provide basically a technical function with minimal contact and little relationship work with the client. The real challenge is to stay on the boundary, to stay at the point where acceptance is never totally denied. The consultant in this instance is always viewed as the "outsider" but becoming "one of the family."

Consultant training: Building up the "emotional muscle"

I have hypothesized that the consultant's role—particularly for the external consultant, but to some extent for the internal consultant too—is a marginal role. The effective consultant is one who operates at the boundary and maintains the boundary position. When key consultative issues confronting the personal needs and desires of the consultant—e.g., involvement, responsibility, and acceptance—are resolved in a way that takes the consultant from the boundary, the effectiveness of the consultant's role is diminished. Training for consultation should include the skills and personal development that involve the resolution of these issues in ways which reinforce the boundary position. The personal development of the consultant must include the development of "emotional muscle" so that the stresses, tensions, and conflicts of the position are dealt with or are tolerated so as not to violate the marginal aspects of the role. In a sense the consultant at the boundary faces these existential dilemmas regularly and his or her effectiveness is related to his or her ability to resolve each dilemma as it arises. Personal resolution of these conflicts by adopting behavior which is exclusively rational or exclusively intuitive destroys the boundary position and creates a consulting mode which may be a distortion of reality.

Reference

Ornstein, R. *The psychology of consciousness*. San Francisco: W. H. Freeman, 1972.

Identifying Consultant Anxieties

Arthur M. Freedman

Professional consultants have personal desires they wish to satisfy and objectives they strive to realize. This is axiomatic for internal and external consultants, for full-time entrepreneurs, and for part-time, university- or institution-based practitioners.

Some examples of these desires and objectives include the following: prestige; appreciation; reputation; future consultation business; money; personal-professional growth (testing limits, expanding/stretching competencies); acquisition of practical material for teaching/publication; validation of own conceptual/procedural models; and greater depth of experience within one circumscribed area of expertise.

Many consultants choose to avoid or keep these issues hidden from their clients; others choose to be explicit and openly discuss what they want to derive from the client and the planned change effort for themselves. Clearly, how the consultant manages his or her desires and objectives with clients will affect both *initial contacts* and *terminations* of consultative relations. For example, if the consultant's greatest desire is to be appreciated and highest priority is money, during the initial contact the consultant is likely to agree to anything the client system spokesperson suggests. Further, such a consultant is likely to try to delay or forestall termination.

Consultants earn their livelihood by demonstrating that they, like most other people, have something valuable to offer—"help." Consultants are, in fact, professional helpers. Consultants are also anxious people. Barry Oshry, a professional helper who seems to operate about six years ahead of most of the rest of us, once discussed and described the issue at a workshop for mental health professionals.

We are all helpers. Some of us help people whom we refer to as "patients." Others of us help those who help those we call "patients." Helpers are anxious people. At some level or another, at one time or another, we are anxious about *whether or not we really have whatever it takes to really "help."* Some level of anxiety is necessary for us to want to do anything; too much anxiety is dysfunctional; too little leads to no movement at all. We have to *manage* our anxiety. We tend to "handle" our anxiety either by trying to *reduce or eliminate* it or by learning to *live with and use* it.

Some relevant dimensions of anxiety-management behavior that consultants seem to choose include the following:

LOOK GOOD; APPEAR COMPETENT BY RESTRICTING ATTENTION TO WHAT YOU KNOW AND DO WELL	BE REAL; SOMETIMES COMPETENCE MEANS WILLINGNESS TO COME TO GRIPS WITH THE UNKNOWN
CREATE AS MUCH CLARITY AS SOON AS POSSIBLE	ACCEPT AND LIVE WITH AMBIGUITY UNTIL YOU UNDERSTAND
AVOID EVIDENCE OF MISTAKES (USE "JIC'S ["JUST IN CASE"] AND "CYA'S [COVER YOUR ASS"]	TAKE RISKS; MANAGING ERRORS MODELS EFFECTIVE PROBLEM SOLVING
DO YOUR OWN THING, WHAT YOU DO BEST	EXPERIMENT WITH NEW ISSUES, CONCEPTS AND METHODS
CREATE (OR BUY) A RIGID PLAN OR DESIGN EVERYTHING BEFORE ANYTHING HAPPENS	DESIGN INCREMENTALLY; WAIT FOR AN EMERGENT PLAN
MAINTAIN CONTROL OVER CLIENTS	SHARE CONTROL WITH CLIENTS
RELY ON TRADITION, OTHERS' THEORIES, AND METHODS	TRUST YOUR OWN AND CLIENT MEMBERS' FEELINGS, IDEAS, AND OBSERVATIONS
STRENGTH IS NO WEAKNESS	WEAKNESS IS NO STRENGTH
STRENGTH IS WEAKNESS	WEAKNESS IS STRENGTH

These dimensions neither describe nor differentiate between "good" and "bad" consultants. Rather, consultants must and do choose helping behaviors which are *comfortable* for and *compatible* with them. Consultants must, but do not always, choose behaviors which enhance their potential to meet the challenge posed by the particular consultative situation by which they are confronted. Many consultants continuously choose the same concepts and methods whatever the situation. What might be appropriate under conditions of one configuration of *people, focal and underlying issues, emotional culture, type of enterprise,* and *organizational structure* might not work under a different set of conditions where some variables are similar (e.g., people and type of enterprise) but others are different or have changed over time (e.g., issues, emotional culture and organizational structure).

Managing Anxieties as a Process Consultant

Robert J. Lee

An important attraction of OD and process consulting as a vocation is the opportunity to become personally involved in meaningful human and organizational experiences. The process consultant has a chance to rise above the minutia, the usual game playing, the content, and touch the essential underlying processes that allow a system to work effectively.

This is not easy work. It requires maintaining a sense of personal balance and perspective beyond what is expected from professionals in many other fields. The process consultant lives within a social system but is not a "regular" part of it. The process consultant is doing things that frequently threaten her or his continued acceptance, or that reduce or eliminate the system's need for this kind of help. Perpetually a guest or a visitor rather than a member of the family, the process consultant has chosen this role because it is gratifying personally and professionally. But it is also quite taxing to forever be walking a tightrope, to be living on the tense edge of change.

How does someone keep personal perspective and balance while in this fiddler-on-the-slippery-roof role? Where does the data come from that tells you which way to lean or move so that you can stay constructively marginal? What are the sources of learning and anxiety that matter to the consultant's efforts to do a good job, grow as a person, and feel good in this unusual role?

There are self-evaluations: short-term ones about how well the actual consulting transactions are going, and long-term ones about whether the consulting is helping to move you along a desired career/life path. There are client evaluations of many kinds: comments, observable successes and failures, referrals, changes in resistance to or acceptance of your role, raised or lowered consulting goals, and so on. Often there are evaluations from peers, supervisors or subordinates who understand what you are trying to do and how well you're doing it. Important feedback also comes from family and friends who know something about your work but a lot more about your total life. Keeping in good contact with these various sources of potential learning and anxiety is a task by itself. It is easy to lose that contact.

A consultant uses the data from these evaluatons to maintain personal perspective. If the feedback leads to learning about oneself and about the actual consulting transaction, then perspective is being maintained. If there is too much anxiety and not enough learning, then the perspective shifts and balance becomes precarious.

You will know that trouble is brewing when perspective and focus have shifted from the actual consulting transactions to one party alone: either too much on yourself as a person, or too much on the inner workings of the client system. Every consultant has his or her own sense of history and internal turmoil to deal with—self-interests, embarrassments, deficiencies, security and approval needs, and so on. Every client has its confusions and resistances about its problems. Balance has been lost when you're working on your own concerns at the client's expense, or when you've been co-opted by the clients into playing their power games or doing their managerial work. These kinds of things happen as short-term ways to reduce the anxiety caused by too much negative feedback from the evaluation sources.

Listed below are some ways to deal with excess negative feedback and anxiety and allow yourself to regain personal perspective and balance.

1. Reduce the number and variety of consulting engagements. Say "no" to a few people; avoid overwork. Put more effort into doing a smaller number of things well.

2. Make greater use of support groups as outlets, mirrors, pillows, and resources.

3. Get someone you respect to serve as a consultant to you.

4. Do some career/life planning with your family. Try to be clear about your own self-interests and how you plan to achieve them. Check to assure that your aspirations are realistic.

5. Try to get as much constructive criticism as you can from the clients, peers, boss, subordinates, and other available sources of evaluative feedback.

6. Whenever possible, choose to work on projects that are useful for your own learning because of how they fit your self-interests and because they can give you useful feedback on your success. Make that learning an explicit part of the client contract and not a hidden agenda.

7. Identify your personal clues as to when your perspective has shifted from the actual consulting transaction to either your own internal turmoil or the client's confusions and resistances. Some clues might be over-reliance on the same instruments or techniques as cure-alls, a sense of obsolescence, jamming of calendar dates, too many "deja vu" feelings, excessively dependent clients, or hearing yourself complain too often.

Checklist for Institutional Sexism

Cultural stereotypes typically become institutionalized in organizations to some degree. Several sex-related stereotypes that often occur in the workplace are listed below.

Individual perceptions

Circle the number which indicates your perception of the degree with which each indicator operates in your organization, using this scale:

1 = Very little or none
2 = Sometimes, but not generally
3 = Frequently, more often than not
4 = Consistently present, few exceptions

1. **Sex-typing of positions.** Are most positions held predominantly by one sex?   1 2 3 4

2. **Different entry jobs (or levels) for women and men.** Do most men enter the system through certain positions and/or at certain levels which differ from where women enter the system?   1 2 3 4

3. **The invisible ceiling.** In each department, is there a job level at which there are one or two women, with virtually none at higher levels?   1 2 3 4

4. **Different meanings of "qualified."** Are women expected to have more education, or more experience, or to "prove themselves" longer than men, or to "prove themselves" under different conditions than men?   1 2 3 4

5. **Different rates of promotion.** Are men promoted faster than women? If women train male bosses but aren't offered the job, this indicates faster promotion rates for men.   1 2 3 4

6. **Different supports while proving oneself.** Do men prove their potential with supports of announced promotion, status symbols, information resources and staff; while women prove themselves prior to promotion without similar supports, using influence rather than formalized authority?   1 2 3 4

7. **Different access to training and development.** Are more dollars expended for men to support their studies, research, or activities in professional organizations; or is more thoroughness given to men in on-the-job learning, including organizational influence systems; or are men given more informal sponsorship ties?   1 2 3 4

8. **Tokenism or "show-case" women.** Are women at the "invisible ceiling" cited as examples that discrimination does not exist, that they are ones who have "made it," implying that others could if they tried, or were capable? This stance may be reinforced by the "token" women.   1 2 3 4

9. **Differences in "whittling" the position size.** "Whittling" occurs when a person is given a position definition of her or his responsibilities and authority, only to find it gradually "whittled" because bits and pieces have been given to others. Does this happen more to positions filled by women than by men?   1 2 3 4

10. **Differences in visability.** Do positions held by women have less public contact, or have less visible involvement in internal affairs, e.g., participation in policy meetings?   1 2 3 4

11. **Differences in influence groups.** Are women represented on company committees, task groups, and advisory groups in proportion to their numbers in the organization?   1 2 3 4

12. **Differences in pay.** Looking at actual work responsibility and skills required, as well as titles, do women receive compensation equivalent to men doing the same work?   1 2 3 4

13. **Differences in communication.** Are there significant differences in how men and women communicate with each vs. with their own sex, and particularly in areas like giving feedback, disagreeing with, being "straight" with, and so on?   1 2 3 4

14. **Double standards.** Do men have different standards for men and women in areas like use of first names, flattery, touching, strong or profane language, and the like?   1 2 3 4

Ethical Issues in OD Intervention*

Matthew B. Miles

OD is an intervention strategy being used more and more widely, by more and more professional practitioners. Most professionals have ethical standards. But so far there has been very little *discussion* of the ethical problems involved in the practice of OD.

This paper first defines OD's core ideas, as I view them, and then outlines a view of what "intervention" means in OD terms, supplementing this with examples of intervention types. The remainder of the paper suggests a series of ethical issues discernible before, during, and after OD intervention, illustrated with examples from my own and others' experience where possible. Some suggestions for improved resolution of ethical issues are made.

My own background and experience with OD includes initiation of the first OD work with schools (1963), accompanied by research on the effort; the Cooperative Project for Educational Development, a similar but more extensive effort; work as an outside change agent in a number of industrial and educational OD efforts; assembling a book on research studies of educational OD (Miles & Schmuck, 1971); work on the staff of NTL's training program for OD practitioners; and a state-of-the-art study of educational OD (Fullan, Miles & Taylor, 1978) which includes a literature review, national surveys of consultants and school districts, and case studies. I do not pretend to have thought through the ethical issues involved in the practice of OD, as I suspect is true for most practitioners and researchers, for whom moral dilemmas surface only fitfully and occasionally when the demands of a particular project highlight them. Further, I suspect that, like myself, well-trained OD professionals are mostly philosophically illiterate when it comes to ethical issues, lacking the sort of coherent framework for thought outlined by Sieber (in press).

At present, the only available systematic discussion of ethics in the OD domain is that by Walton and Warwick (1973). This paper draws heavily on their work (which has also generated two separate chapters: Walton, 1978; Warwick, 1978), and on the more general discussion of social intervention appearing in Bermant, Kelman, and Warwick (1978).

*From *OD Practitioner*, Vol. 11, No. 3, 1979, a publication of the OD Network. Used by permission.

Definition of OD

OD is a strategy for organizational improvement dating from approximately 1954. In such a young field, definitions have proliferated almost endlessly; issues of the *OD Practitioner* have included articles with such titles as "What is OD? No More Definitions, Please!" and "How Do You Know It Works if You Don't Know What It is?" A comprehensive review (Fullan, Miles & Taylor, 1978) concluded that the key components of OD were

(1) deliberate planned change effort;
(2) long-range extent (usually several years);
(3) emphasis on improving both organizational functioning[1] and quality of individuals' work lives;
(4) use of internal and external change agents to assist the process;
(5) application of behavioral science concepts;
(6) reflexive, self-analytic approach involving the organization's members in data collection, diagnosis, and action directed toward improvement.

We should note that OD fits the general class of change strategies reviewed by Bermant, Kelman and Warwick (1978): it is deliberate, it involves a somewhat professionalized change-agent, it utilizes the ideas of social science, and it is "benign," aiming at supporting and improving its client systems.

Some typical interventions

Some typical OD interventions, arranged in rough order from "soft" (person-changing) to "hard" (task-oriented or structure-changing) are the following:

Training or education: procedures involving direct teaching or experience-based learning. Examples:

[1]Typical organizational issues addressed include leadership, problem-solving, communication, trust, conflict and similar "human processes," along with technostructural issues (work flow, role definition, technology). These issues may be focused on at relatively micro levels (person, role, dyadic or triadic relationship), or (more typically) at the group, intergroup, or total-organizational level.

lectures, exercises, simulations, and T Groups.

Process consultation: watching and aiding ongoing processes and coaching to improve them.

Confrontation: bringing together units of the organization (persons, roles, or groups) which have previously been in poor communication; usually accompanied by supporting data.

Data feedback: systematic collection of information, which is then reported back to appropriate organizational units as a base for diagnosis, problem solving, and planning.

Problem solving: meetings essentially focusing on problem identification, diagnosis, and invention and implementation.

Plan making: activity focused primarily on goal setting to replot the organization's future.

OD task-force establishment: setting up ad hoc problem-solving groups or internal teams of specialists to ensure that the organization solves problems and carries out plans continuously.

Technostructural activity: action which has as its prime focus the alteration of the organization's structure, work-flow, and means of accomplishing tasks.

These interventions are not mutually exclusive; most programs will typically involve a mix of them. Nor is the list exhaustive: OD practitioners use a wide range of other interventions, ranging from "role bargaining" to "life planning," and verge over into work on "job enrichment," "management by objectives," "socio-technical-systems planning" and adaptations of Gestalt therapy.

I define intervention, in the OD context, as an intentional effort to reorient existing processes (and supporting structures) in an organization in order to enhance organizational "capacity" or "health."[2] We might usefully compare this with some other definitions.

Bermant, Kelman and Warwick (1978) call social intervention

Any act, planned or unplanned, that alters the characteristics of another individual or the pattern of relationships between individuals.

and then refine this further to:

Deliberate attempts by professionals to change the

characteristics of individuals or groups, or to influence the pattern of relationships between individuals and/or groups.

My definition takes the characteristics of OD (use of change-agents, social science concepts, reflexiveness, etc.) as unstated givens, and focuses further on a special class of change (capacity development).

Argyris (1970) defines intervention as:

To enter into an ongoing system for relationships, to come between or among persons, groups, or objects for the purpose of helping them. There is an important explicit assumption in the definition that should be made explicit: the system exists independently of the intervenor.

An intervenor...assists a system to become more effective in problem solving, decision making, and decision implementation in such a way that the system can continue to be increasingly effective in these activities and have a decreasing need for the intervenor.

Argyris suggests further that certain basic processes must be fulfilled if an intervention activity is to be "help-ful": the generation of valid information, the presence of free and informed choice, and internal commitment by the client to the choices made. He denies that intervention should necessarily be aimed at "change" in the organization, preferring to focus on the primary tasks named above (i.e., an organization, given good information, choice and commitment, might decide not to change, to reaffirm its stability, etc.). But that seems to me to miss the point that achieving the three primary tasks is itself a change: important organizational processes have been reoriented.

The "capacity" or "health" part of my definition suffers from vagueness. Since the "development" part of OD implies some sort of desirable (or possibly "natural," "matured") end state of a system, OD practitioners need to be explicit about what it is they consider good. Argyris has done so with the three primary tasks. I have suggested (Miles, 1965) 10 major dimensions of a healthy organization: goal focus, communication adequacy, optimal power equalization, resource utilization, cohesiveness, morale, innovativeness, autonomy, adaptation, and problem-solving adequacy. A healthy organization, in my view,

not only survives in its environment, but continues over the long haul, and continuously develops and extends its surviving and coping abilities. Short-run operations on any particular day may be effective or ineffective, but continued survival, adequate coping and growth are taking place.

(Note that this sort of definition leaves aside the question of the organization's goals, just as a definition of personal health leaves aside the question of whether the person's activities are criminal or law-abiding, politically right or left, etc.)

[2]Adapted from Miles and Schmuck (1971).

Weisbord (1977), noting that many OD practitioners have acted as if their mission were to produce "Theory Y" (collaborative) managers, or to emphasize matters such as increased participation, autonomy, and "humaneness," suggests in contrast that OD's "right goal" should be that of enabling organization members to confront two basic dilemmas: the tension between freedom and constraint, and the relationship between substantive tasks and organizational processes. That is, more freedom or more process orientation is not the issue, but being aware of the tension, and (in Argyris's terms) helping people to use valid data, make free choices, and take committed action to resolve it, is the core. In this sense, Weisbord comes down strongly on the side of an inquiring, self-analytic stance as the crucial one to aim for. This sort of definition is important, because it suggests that core values (notably rationalism, autonomy, truth, and freedom) are at stake, and that certain other values (notably justice, "humaneness," equity) remain moot.[3]

Ethical issues in OD intervention

Though a "profession" is usually defined as a collection of persons using specialized knowledge in the service of clients, and bound by a code of ethics, the most striking thing about most professions is the rarity with which ethical issues are (a) explicitly discussed; (b) treated with awareness during the conduct of practice; (c) used as a basis for sanctions against deviant behavior.[4]

OD is an emerging profession. There is as yet no formulated ethics code (the International Association of Applied Social Scientists is now taking the first steps to formulate one). As indicated earlier, only Walton and Warwick (1973) have tried to identify ethical issues publicly. There have been a number of discussions of more general value issues (see Fullan, Miles & Taylor, 1978, for a review), but a scan of the last few years' issues of the *OD Practitioner* and a number of recent texts yields nothing at all on the specific ethical dilemmas—the goods and bads of daily OD practice—which those carrying out OD are confronted with. Walton and Warwick's article produced no letters to the *Journal of Applied Behavioral Science*. Perhaps the usual professional avoidance of ethical issues is enhanced by the need to extend and solidify the professional role of the OD practitioner.

There is no coherent way to organize the range of ethical issues appearing in connection with OD programs. I will sort them for the moment into five general categories: issues appearing prior to the OD program, and issues relating to the setting of goals, the choice of "targets" for intervention, the choice of intervention means, and the results or effects of OD intervention. As will become clear, there are a number of ethical issues (exercise of choice, provision of full information, assurance of welfare, equity among various actors) which

recur across these categories.

Prior to the OD program

Organization-intervener value congruence. An intervener ought to think of what the organization he or she intends to help is for. While most change-agents would not work for the Ku Klux Klan, a few would. And many (though not all) would work for Dow Chemical. The question is whether one's personal values are congruent with what the organization, if made more "healthy" is set up to accomplish.

Example: The Army Corps of Chaplains wanted an OD program primarily aimed at coping with race prejudice. I did not want to associate myself passively with a organization which was then conducting a war (Vietnam) to which I was opposed. I made it clear that if I were to enter the program I would be working to raise participants' awareness about the undesirability and injustice of the war (and its differential impact on Blacks). The coordinator for the program declined my services.[5]

Doctors (who must heal all who come to them), and lawyers (who are expected to be advocates for someone they personally believe to have done wrong), are freed from this choice. For an OD consultant, the choice to give or withhold aid based on value-congruence issues is present—even when it is denied in the service of a supposedly "neutral" view.

Exaggerated intervener claims. Bowers (1977) and others have pointed out that interveners may, to gain entry and sell their services, make inflated claims for what OD can accomplish. This amounts to misrepresentation of services to be offered.

The choice to launch an OD program. The decision to begin an OD program is characteristically made by a small group of managers, usually at the top of the system, and one or more consultants. Even within this limited group, the question is whether anything like "informed consent" has taken place. Did the choosers have full information about the possible and probable

[3]See also Friedlander's (1978) interesting discussion of the rationalist, pragmatist, and existentialist (person-oriented) roots of OD and the difficulties involved in effective blending of these value orientations.

[4]For example, the American Psychological Association has a well-developed code of ethics (APA, 1963), but in a membership of over 30,000 persons, ethical violations are usually officially cited for less than a half dozen persons each year. Yet APA members are not saints; all 30,000 in fact (if they allow it into awareness) are faced with ethical issues daily, and their decisions must certainly not conform with the code at all times.

[5]The reader will undoubtedly be able to notice ethical issues in this (and later) examples other than the ones mentioned.

costs along with the benefits? Were they able to make a free and uncoerced choice?

> Example: A manager wanted a program to "improve communication" among his immediate subordinates. I recommended a team-building session that would involve him and them directly in discussing their working relationships. I described the proposed intervention and explained that he would undoubtedly receive much feedback on his own behavior, and that it might be painful. He decided to proceed.

In this case, nominal information was provided. But as Bermant and Warwick (1978) point out, the power of the external change-agent can be quite high because of specialized expertise and/or prestige, the need of clients for help, etc. The manager may have been less than wholly free in making the choice.

Entry to an OD program as described above also leaves out the question of how much participation other affected parties—such as subordinates—have in the decision to proceed. This dilemma is not wholly solved by mechanisms of widespread participation in the launch decision. A frequent phenomenon when a larger group is asked to make the entry decision is that the very problems (e.g., mistrust, inability to make decisions, unresolved conflict) for which the OD program is a proposed remedy, surface and successfully block decision. Thus capacity to make a good decision may be lacking.

Goal-Setting

Whose interests are to be served? This question has several parts. First, the goals for OD work may serve the intervener's interests, as versus those of the system—(i.e., they may be chosen so as to maximize income to the intervener, or a chance to test his or her pet theories, follow a special interest, provide work for associates or students, or enhance the power of the OD function if the intervener is an inside change-agent. The question is whether such intervener interests are acknowledged, or left unexpressed, with the pretense that only system interests matter.

A second issue is which parts of the system will have their interests met.

Example: A top management group defined "the problem" as one of indifference by first-line foremen, and asked for a program to improve motivation. Top managers also considered that foremen had few productive ideas for improvement. A colleague and I said we believed the foremen probably had a different story to tell, and proposed a problem-solving project in which foremen would diagnose and provisionally solve problems. Managers would do the same separately after which the two groups would merge for joint problem solving. The foremen's interests (e.g., overload reduction) proved to be different in many respects from those of managers, but they were far from indifferent, and joint problem solving was productive.

This is a good illustration of the basic point made by Mirvis and Seashore (in press):

> Most ethical dilemmas in organizational research arise not from personal immorality, but from the researcher becoming entangled in a network of multiple roles and in the conflicting expectations derived from them.[6]

A third issue is whether individual or organizational priorities will take precedence. While much OD language speaks of the "quality of work life," "individual needs," "Theory Y," etc., the fact is that management ordinarily pays for OD, and is preoccupied with whether the intervention will increase organizational effectiveness, output, efficiency, etc. It is quite rare to hear an OD consultant say as frankly as Pagés does

> I do not have goals for the organization, except probably to destroy it. I do not want to work for organizations any more; I want to work for people...my main wish *IS NOT* to comfort the organization, *NOT* to try to reach a new equilibrium....I want to work more on mobilizing people's wants. I think what people individually and psychologically (even unconsciously) want is something which is *SOCIAL*; they want a different kind of relationship with people. They want to have the opportunity to express their needs and to be able to pursue them. They want not to be bossed; they want to enter into relationships that will not be possessive. This is what I wish to mobilize when I work with people. (Tichy, 1974)

A more typical note is from Petrella (1977):

> Most organizations are "about" output and productivity. How satisfied people are in their work is really a secondary value....If you want to be shown the exit, start talking about humanizing work or the quality of working life without showing that you are deeply concerned about productivity....Yet I see OD as trying to do something that will find a new balance (between individual and organization) in the work setting.

And a final issue of whose interests will be served is more general: will the OD program bring about changes, or serve the status quo? Though the rhetoric of OD programs is usually for "planned change," sponsorship by top management (a requisite most observers agree is essential) may often mean that little real shift occurs in such matters as power distribution, the conditions of work, or compensation: the latent function of the OD program is to co-opt and cool out "disruptive" forces, and stabilize, affirm, and strengthen the existing order.

> I have found that many OD consultants, employed by members of management for use in their organizations, seem actually to function as re-stabilizing agents rather than change agents. Their real purpose within the organization is not to foster growth and improvement but rather to restore a lost homeostatic balance.[7] (Forbes, 1977)

More generally and even more harshly, we should note Lundberg's (1978) comment:

> Most of OD's assumptions (rules of thumb?) would have us uncritically accept a capitalist economic and political structure, uncritically adjust to economic and technological growth, and uncritically accept the importance of social class and the centrality of work in people's lives. Most OD "assumptions" blind theorizers to the differences and pluralism of organizations and the real, structural sources of conflict.

And, we might add, blind them to the fact that modern organizations, even at their most enlightened, are systems full of inequity and coercion, institutionalized in such a way that injustice and compulsion are not quite noticed. It takes a Sam Goldwyn to bring this to our attention ("I want a man who will say 'no' to me, even if he gets fired for it.")

How goals are set

Beneath all these issues of the various interests served by OD are questions of how explicitly and fully various conflicting interests are allowed to surface and engage each other, and the relative power of the various parties involved in goal-setting decisions. There is typically a temptation to leave such issues implicit and unquestioned, and for consultants to employ their power as external experts while allying themselves with the formal power of top management, so that the interests of less powerful parts of the client system are less fully represented.

Conceptual mapping

This term sounds ethically neutral, but the implicit cognitive maps of change-agents—given the extra loading that expertise enables—serve, very often, to define OD programs' goals in restrictive ways. As Bermant and Warwick (1978) sarcastically point out:

> The intervenor's most important task is defining the problem to be solved in a way that minimizes impediments to solution. In particular, the intervenor should define the problem so as to forestall the need to justify the intervention. If one does not have to explain why intervention is

[6]In passing, I commend Mirvis and Seashore's work, especially that on the need to build role relationships capable of "addressing" and moderating ethical dilemmas that are not, and cannot, be covered by prescription.
[7]Change-agents sometimes virtuously point out that not intervening at all also has the effect of maintaining the status quo (and thus, one should at least try). I am alluding here, however, to a more insidious process: allowing (or tacitly choosing) the movement of OD programs toward system maintenance as against other considerations (such as equity, justice, or the need for radical change).

necessary, one can move quickly to consider how to accomplish it.

Thus, implicit notions of "organizational health," and—as Tichy and Hornstein (1976) have vividly shown—one's selection of just which organizational variables are "important," salient, and changeable—are very powerful in OD planning. Explicitness about them is desirable.

Data collection and feedback

Typically, goal-setting and diagnosis stem from some form of more-or-less systematic data collection in the organization. Certain issues typically arise. One is, of course, confidentiality. Will individuals who provide data be identified later on during the program?

> Example: I usually begin data-collection interviews with the admonition that if there is anything the person wants to say, but wishes kept "off the record," he or she should so indicate. Otherwise data are to be treated as public. This develops trust (which cannot be lightly breached later), but may also place the consultant in a difficult position (knowing about sensitive information which he or she is powerless to use directly in the intervention).

> A colleague takes a different tack: "Anything you tell me is on the record." This requires the respondent to censor her or himself.

Even with such ground rules, it is easy for OD participants, carried away by the chance to talk about problems that may have been troubling them for some time, to reveal more than they realize, with potentially damaging results for them (or others) when data are reported back.[8]
There is also the allied question of privacy. People (and indeed groups) should have the right to a protected area where certain behavior, thoughts, and feelings can remain inviolable, free from scrutiny. That individuals (and groups) define this area somewhat idiosyncratically (some persons easily and willingly discuss matters that others regard as personal and private) does not obscure this right.
Finally, when data collected during early goal-setting and diagnostic activities are fed back, there are questions of the completeness of feedback, and the extensiveness of the audience. Any summary is, of course, partial, but the ethical issue is whether the primary material presented is full or distorted (for any number of noble or nefarious reasons). One can argue that material which should be

[8]Walton and Warwick (1973) report examples in which managers requested information from OD consultants about subordinates' responses as an aid in making personnel decisions. This is easy to refuse (if one's prior commitment to confidentiality has been clear). But what if the subordinate is actually quite incompetent and deserves to be fired, in the consultant's opinion, and the superior is genuinely unaware of the situation?

"unnecessarily" painful to individuals, or is harmful to their interests, or deals with an issue about which no constructive action can conceivably be taken, should be excised. OD change-agents usually make such decisions intuitively and quickly, but they are not minor decisions at all. There is the associated question of who should receive data feedback. The ordinary commitment is that all those who provided data should. But circumstances can arise that inhibit this.

> Example: In a research project, I reviewed survey data from a school faculty with the principal, prior to making a summary for feedback to the teachers. He insisted that data bearing on the presence of certain problems be deleted because they would make him look bad with the central office. I agreed, because I wanted to maintain the research relationship, which had not had an OD-like, system-improving aspect. Nevertheless, the data reported to the teachers gave an incomplete picture.

Diagnostic quality

The question here is ultimately one of OD practitioner competence: are the problems identified for action the "correct" ones? The issue is far less clear than in, say, medical diagnosis, where a ruptured appendix will clearly prove a diagnosis of temporary gastritis to have been mistaken. The point is partly that (if they are allowed in) there are many conflicting parties to the diagnostic struggle, and many possible versions of what is wrong, or what has to be fixed or augmented. It is also true that organizational diagnosis is still a somewhat arbitrary and intuitively practiced art. Under these circumstances, OD practitioners have a clear obligation to be sure that their own "preferred diagnosis" (such as mistrust, lack of group skills, or power maldistribution) are not prevailing, that data from many different parties are included, and that minority opinions are zealously pursued for the light they can shed.

The targets of change

In most OD programs, the people whose behavior and work life will be changed by OD programs ("targets") are a larger set than the people who decided to begin the program ("clients" or "sponsors"). The question of who will be changed interacts closely with the question of the goals of the OD program, so the issues noted above all apply. I concur with Bermant and Warwick (1978), who point out that the alliance of the sponsor with the OD consultant (who has strong expert power derived from her or his general image, actual expert knowledge, and skills drawn from past work) produces a decidedly asymmetrical power relationship with the targets of change, who in addition to the sponsor will typically include the sponsor's subordinates.

Thus questions of how much "say" the targets of change have in the very decision to designate them as targets and the character of the "informed consent" involved in their decision to participate in intervention events are quite crucial. As Walton and Warwick (1973) have pointed out, even where superiors do not require subordinates to participate in an OD intervention, saying that attendance is "voluntary," the fact of power difference is real: subordinates may not have a genuine choice to decline. Group conformity effects can exert pressure as well. The paradox, of course, is that OD is committed both to free choice and to the idea that all parties to a problematic situation need to be involved in diagnosing and improving it. But if someone exercises a choice not to participate, then full-scale work is jeopardized. And, if someone is, even gently, coerced to participate in the name of "full involvement," then the principle of choice has been compromised.

The means of intervention

Choosing intervention means

This area at first blush looks "technical": does the practitioner choose the "right" intervention (one which will deal effectively with the diagnosis and which will not have unwanted side effects)? But there are clearly ethical issues as well. As Walton and Warwick (1973) point out, many early OD practitioners came from a background as human relations (T-Group) trainers. They concluded that T Groups carried out in an organizational setting were a good intervention method. But (a) this intervention was often not differentially related to or matched with organizational issues, so a sort of monolithic prescription was involved; (b) the intensity of T-Group methods had undesirable side effects (such as polarization) when carried out with colleague groups; (c) the choice of this intervention focused primary attention on interpersonal issues, often to the detriment of attention to structural matters, intergroup conflict, physical technology, and the like. The first such misapplication of in-organization T Groups could simply be called a function of consultant inexperience or incompetence. But continuing to prescribe such an intervention once such effects were known would be decidedly unethical.

Walton and Warwick (1973) also point out that early OD consultants often chose intervention means that were quite time-limited, with minimal long-term attention to follow-up and support. Bowers (1978) also notes that superficial intervention means may be proposed and carried out, with minimal consultant commitment to long-term developmental effort. There is now enough evidence about the length of time (two years plus) required for effective OD work that interventions with a shorter time scale, as Fullan, Miles and Taylor (1978) suggest, should probably not be labelled "OD," but perhaps "OT" for "organizational training." What is at stake here is a matter, once again, of the OD consultant's promises, coupled with the likelihood that they can in fact be achieved.

The choice to enter (or depart) from an intervention

We have already reviewed some of the issues inherent in the decision to embark on an OD program. These recur when the issue is a particular intervention—such as a team-building workshop, a survey feedback design, or indeed, a particular exercise in the context of a larger intervention.

> Example: I explained a particular micro-intervention aimed at organizational diagnosis (the participants, divided into groups by their organizational role, would draw a picture of the organization in any symbolic way they chose). I had earlier explained that anyone who did not want to participate could "sit it out." No one did so. One group drew a picture of the organization, a college, as a large, donkey-like animal. The president's initials were placed by the animal's eyes. The president's assistant was a strong, able woman, and her initials were placed by the animal's brain and its testicles. The group was communicating its view of the president, but in a way that was quite painful.

In this case, "sitting out" the intervention was relatively meaningless. And it is likely that even if I had explained more about the potential costs (as well as the benefits) of the activity (and its essential unpredictability), people would not have been able to make a meaningful choice as to whether or not to take part.

As Walton and Warwick (1973) point out, leaving an intervention, once it is under way, is difficult even if "permission" has been given; such departures usually alarm other group members (and sometimes the consultant), and pressure is exerted on the member to stay, often in the name of providing support, but sometimes with the effect of intensifying the difficulties which led the person to wish to leave in the first place.

Influence mode of interventions

Interventions are by my definition aimed at "reorienting" processes and structures, at bringing about change. The question is what mode of influence the intervention utilizes. Here I follow Kelman and Warwick (1978): the intervention may involve coercion (threats of deprivation to induce an action that would not be undertaken willingly); manipulation (restriction of choice, often without full awareness); persuasion (argument, reasoning, etc.); or facilitation (aiding the achievement of individual or group desires).

Coercion, in a strict sense, is rare within OD interventions, even though, as I have noted, subordinates may feel coerced to take part in particular interventions. And though most OD consultants reject coercive interventions

as being inherently opposed to OD's "true nature" (collaborative, self-analytic problem-solving), this does not rule out the fact that particular micro-interventions may be perceived by participants as coercive, either because the structure of the design seems to require behavior they would not willingly produce, or because they fear retaliation from superiors if they do not participate. In my view, the consultant's responsibility is to monitor interventions carefully for the possibility that they are having coercive effects, and to making participant exit (and counterinfluence) easy.

OD interventions rarely involve what Kelman and Warwick call "psychic manipulation" (for example, deliberate deception, or control of information of which the subject of manipulation in unaware),[9] partly because of OD ideology and partly because such efforts are almost invariably discovered, with deteriorative effects on the relationship between change-agent and "target." But environmental manipulation is a fairly frequent feature of OD interventions. The structure of interventions often serves to restrict choices by participants in ways which are not wholly clear to them, either at the outset or during the intervention itself.

> Example: In a workshop being held with a superintendent, central-office personnel and school principals, one change goal was to clarify the power relationships among those present. The micro-intervention used was a "power ladder." Participants were asked to arrange themselves in a line, with one end reserved for the person who saw him or herself as exerting most influence over what happened in the school district. Persons were asked to make a strict rank-ordering of themselves in relation to others, on the influence dimension. The design did not permit ties, or multiple, lateral influence.
>
> The latter part of the design asked individuals to "rearrange" the line according to their view. A subsequent step asked people to arrange themselves according to the influence structure they desired, without requiring the rank-ordering.
>
> In all cases, the choices were sharply limited by the activity's structure, and some only belatedly realized that the exercise might be painful. A principal who placed himself low on the line had some sharp, recriminatory exchanges with the superintendent ("If this is all the thanks I get after 20 years, I'm leaving.") He left the workshop shortly afterward, even though other participants provided much support.

Persuasive interventions are relatively frequent in OD programs; OD consultants give advice and coaching; they set up situations in which participants can influence each other, often more directly than may have been the case in the past; and they often supply conceptual schemes and material which argues for a particular point of view about "effective" organizations, desirable conditions in group and interpersonal settings, and so on. The

---

[9]Compare Argyris (1970) who defined manipulation as a usually covert effort to influence persons without their awareness of the effort, and/or their realization that the effort is against their interests.

ethical issue may be: is the persuasive effort carried out openly and directly, with full opportunity for the target of the influence effort to resist or withdraw—or is the expert authority of the consultant (or the conformity pressure of the group setting) being tacitly used to stack the deck?

Facilitative interventions are supposedly the primary stock in trade of OD practitioners, who typically define themselves as helping people to get what they want. But there are tricky problems even here: Whose goals are being considered (those of the manager?) and what are the consequences of supporting movement toward them? Sometimes the choice to facilitate becomes essentially a paternalistic one, so that the system may have been not at all "strengthened" or "developed" in the process.

Example: In a research project to which I was a consultant, a junior member complained bitterly in a small-group diagnostic session that certain decision-making structures were unclear to him. He also felt quite unsure about raising the issue with the complete project staff. Since his uncertainties affected the immediate future of the project, I proposed a confrontation meeting between him and the project managers.

At the meeting, the managers felt somewhat surprised and a bit threatened by the confrontation, saying that they had expected to get to the clarification very soon anyway. The junior member was seen as having overdramatized the issue, and as not having surfaced it earlier. These perceptions were only partially correct, because the "confrontation" had been created through my initiative and "managing." It is not clear whether the junior member and the managers learned to deal with future uncertainties more effectively.

The results of OD intervention

Harmfulness

Since OD programs usually involve the increased flow of information in a system and often lead to shifts in the influence process, it is almost impossible to guarantee that there will be no negative effects. Information will become public that its owners had wished were kept private; some participants' influence will rise and others' will drop. Specific decisions may be made during OD programs that work against an individual's or a group's best interests. All this is true in ordinary organizational life, of course. But when an organization and the people in it function more effectively and satisfyingly, there is an extra burden: OD interventions should (at the least) be no more harmful to persons and systems than the ordinary events and processes in daily life and work.

Even in the short run, this guideline presents difficulties. (In the "power ladder" activity above, for example, was the increased clarity achieved about existing influence relationships, and the shared vision of how those relationships needed improvement sufficient justification for the pain to the specific principle involved?) And the long-run issues are not minor either.

Example: A few months later the superintendent decided to fire the principal. Though he told me shortly after the "power ladder" experience that he had been pessimistic about the principal's performance for some time, the possibility cannot be ruled out that the OD intervention accelerated his decision. (It may have slowed it too: the other principals' support during the intervention may have encouraged him to give the principal the benefit of the doubt.)

Here the interests of an individual and of the organization are potentially in conflict, and an action, which may have been stimulated by an OD intervention, resulted in what the individual would deem to be harmful.

Unintended negative effects

According to data (Miles, Fullan & Taylor, 1978) OD programs, like other programs, have some effects that are both unexpected and negative. That these efforts (such as overload, polarization, resistance to the program itself) are usually not serious, and do not detract from the overall satisfaction of OD's users, does not resolve the issue at hand: such effects can be expected though not precisely predicted.

Example: Working as an inside change-agent to an academic organization, I set up a diagnostic and problem-solving meeting in which faculty members participated with great enthusiasm.

One part of their diagnosis was that the organization needed more decisive management. The present manager was respected as a capable researcher, but the faculty wanted more active problem solving and organizational leadership from him. He acknowledged this and set plans in motion including a revised approach to faculty meetings, a steering group, and other mechanisms. They seemed successful.

The manager resigned the following year. Much later I was told that the meeting had left "scars" for him and for others. I inferred that the feedback to the manager had lowered his self-esteem, and reduced his willingness to continue as manager, though this had not been apparent at the time, nor during the subsequent months.[10]

More generally, as Kelman and Warwick (1978) indicate, it is important for change-agents to anticipate that negative effects of intervention may well include such features as the following: suffering of individuals; power losses by one group vis à vis another; weakening of integrative values: heightening of aspirations without corresponding achievement ability; increased dependency on the change-agent.

Accountability

To whom are OD change-agents accountable? At one level, as Bermant and Warwick (1978) point out, they are personally accountable for their actions, like any person in society. They should not lie, cheat, steal, or engage in similar socially reprehensible actions. And they are legally accountable in a very general sense, not only for mis-demeanors and felonies, but for items like breach of contract. However, I have never heard of malpractice litigations being threatened against an OD practitioner (though it has occurred for encounter-group leaders).

In any case, litigation is a gross tool for ensuring ethical behavior by practitioners. The most central form of accountability is that which OD consultants have toward their sponsors, who are paying the bill, in several senses. Sponsors can terminate contracts, or at least revise them, if the program is not functioning as intended. (Once again, this leaves unsolved the question of the consultant's primary "client" and to whom he or she owes loyalty. One can easily envision a situation in which the "sponsor" was satisfied with an OD program which was dubious on one or more ethical grounds.) Such an outcome is far more likely when a consultant has failed to be fully explicit and as anticipatory as possible about whose interests are being served by the relationship:

Only too often, it seems, well-intentioned professionals enter a complex situation without a real understanding of whom they are working for and the potential conflicts of interest that might arise. (Bermant & Warwick, 1978)

Finally, there is professional accountability for OD practitioners, for which at present there are no formal, structural supports comparable to those in medicine, law, accounting, and psychology. As mentioned earlier, this may be in part a function of OD's newness; but it may also be (to take a more cynical view) that professional regulation is weak because society has little data that would suggest OD can do serious harm (or serious good) to organizations or persons.

Bermant and Warwick (1978) suggest that accountability should be directed toward such matters as basic competence of practitioners, truthfulness about expected benefits, protection of confidentiality, and responsibility for indirect or "higher order" effects. I am inclined to agree in principle, but remain pessimistic about accountability structures which are far removed from the basic contractual situation obtaining between client and consultant.

Suggestions

Here I will be quite brief and general, if only because the ethical issues outlined are still somewhat unclear and murky at a number of points.

Increased clarity. The issues outlined here should be worked through, and specified more clearly. Efforts like the current one of IAASS should proceed: codes of ethics, if empirically grounded (like those of APA, for example),

are worthwhile, even if few clear sanctions exist for them, because they increase the salience of ethical issues, and practitioners discuss them, in and out of print.

Client awareness. Users of OD services ought to be made more fully aware of ethical issues involved, partly because they too are typically implicated in the issues, and partly because they are in the best position to exert influence over the behavior of consultants.

The ideas for client "empowerment" suggested by Bermant and Warwick (1978) are also relevant here: clients who have been pre-educated specifically about how OD works and what they may expect are in a better position to exert constructive influence on OD project planning.[11] Client (and target) participation in "threshold" decisions in particular (entering an OD program, planning interventions, shifting to a new phase or target group, etc.) is probably the prime protection against unethical outcomes.

Practitioner awareness. The curricula of OD training programs, and "in-service" events such as the national OD Network meetings, should contain more attention to ethical issues. Articles on ethics, like this one, should appear in professional journals. As Mirvis and Seashore (in press) suggest, by now "naivete about ethics is in itself unethical."

Incremental, piloting mode. Most OD programs use this stance naturally, but issues such as informed consent, full participation in planning, and anticipation of negative effects are much more likely when the first step of OD work involves small-scale pilot work—and prespecification that large-scale work will not proceed until specific classes of data are available from the pilot.

Counter-consultants. Bermant and Warwick (1978) suggest that since OD contracts are entered into by a specially interested party—the consultant—clients are well-advised to retain a counter-consultant, who can critique the work being proposed, the present state of the diagnostic and goal-setting plan, etc., from a detached, third-party position. It should, of course, be stipulated that the counter-consultant may not be subsequently hired by the client. If surgeons can tolerate second opinions, so can OD consultants.

In conclusion, though OD practitioners show few signs of wanting to clarify and promulgate ethical guidelines, more precision about ethics is needed. When we talk about OD, we are talking about the expenditure of a good deal of time and money; and we are talking about an emerging profession which is trying to deal with ancient and near-intractable issues in a competent way. The stakes are not small.

[10]I can also be faulted here for not having stayed in closer touch with the manager following the intervention and for limiting my continued assistance.

[11]For an example of such "pre-education," see C. Phillip Alexander's "The Perils and Pitfalls of an OD Effort: A Manager's Checklist," *OD Practitioner, 11,* 1, 1979.

References

American Psychological Association. *Ethical standards of psychologists*. Washington, D.C.: APA, 1963.

Argyris, C., *Intervention theory and method*. Reading, Mass.: Addison-Wesley, 1970.

Bermant, G., Kelman, H. C., & Warwick, D. P. "The ethics of social intervention: power, freedom and accountability." In Bermant, Kelman and Warwick (Eds.), *The ethics of social intervention*. Washington, D.C.: Hemisphere, 1978. Pp. 377-418.

Bowers, D. G. Organizational development: Promises, performance, possibilities. *Organizational Dynamics*, 1977.

Forbes, R. L., Jr. Organization development: Form or substance? *OD Practitioner*, 9(2) 1977, 12-13.

Friedlander, F. OD reaches adolescence: An exploration of its underlying values. *Journal of Applied Behavioral Science*, 12(1), 1978, 7-21.

Fullan, M., Miles, M. B., & Taylor, B. *OD in schools: The state of the art*. Final Report (5 vols.), National Institute of Education, Contracts 400-77-0051, 0052. Toronto: Ontario Institute for Studies in Education, and New York: Center for Policy Research, 1978.

Kelman, H. C., & Warwick, D. P. The ethics of social intervention: Goals, means and consequences. In Bermant, Kelman and Warwick (Eds.), *The ethics of social intervention*. Washington, D.C.: Hemisphere, 1978. Pp. 3-33.

Lundberg, C. *The current state of theory in organization development*. Paper read at the Academy of Management Meeting, San Francisco, August, 1978.

Miles, M. B., & Schmuck, R. A. Improving schools through organization development: An overview. In R. A. Schmuck & M. B. Miles (Eds.), *Organization development in schools*. La Jolla, Calif.: University Associates, 1971. Pp. 1-27.

Miles, M. B. Planned change and organizational health: Figure and ground. In R. O. Carlson et al., *Change processes in the public schools*. Eugene, Oregon: CASEA, University of Oregon, 1965. Pp. 11-34.

Mirvis, P. H., & Seashore, S. E. Being ethical in organizational research. In J. E. Sieber (Ed.), *Ethical decision-making in social science research* (in press).

Petrella, T. Cold cash, cold logic, and "living in the hollows of our hands," *OD Practitioner*, 1977, 9(4) 2.

Sieber, J. E. Normative ethical theory: Defining the good in behavioral research. In *Methods and Values of Behavioral Resarch* (in press).

Tichy, N. An interview with Max Páges. *Journal of Applied Behavioral Science*, 1974, 10(1), 8-26.

Tichy, N., & Hornstein, H. Stand when your number is called: An empirical attempt to classify types of social change agents. *Human Relations*, 1976, 29(10), 945-967.

Walton, R. E., & Warwick, D. P. Ethical issues in the practice of organization development. In Bermant, Kelman and Warwick (Eds.), *The ethics of social intervention*. Washington, D.C.: Hemisphere, 1978, Pp. 121-145.

Walton, R. E., & Warwick, D. P. The ethics of organization development. *Journal of Applied Behavioral Science*, 1973, 9(6), 681-698.

Warwick, D. P. Moral dilemmas in organization development. In Berman, Kelman and Warwick (Eds.), *The ethics of social intervention*. Washington, D.C.: Hemisphere, 1978. Pp. 147-160.

Weisbord, M. How do you know it works if you don't know what it is? *OD Practitioner*, 1977, 9(3), 1-9.

Affirmative Action: Total Systems Change

ALICE G. SARGENT

Organizations currently take a piecemeal approach to affirmative action. A more effective approach would seek to integrate affirmative action across all organizational planning and management systems. Affirmative action can succeed only if management links it to the following: human resources management, which deals with having the right people at the right place at the right time; an effective performance management system, which includes both career development and appraisal; and the quality of work life, which concerns managing diversity and developing a multicultural work environment. Another approach, characterized by Juanita Kreps, former Secretary of Commerce, calls for "the second bottom line to be corporate social responsibility." The first line is profit; the second is a concern for such social factors as the effective use of human and environmental resources. At their roots, these approaches seek to generate awareness and then change the processes that have systematically failed to use fully our most important resource—people.

Affirmative action is a management problem, and as such proves the effectiveness or lack of it of most management practices within the organization. It spotlights the extent to which organizations make management of human resources a priority. It raises intense interdepartmental issues and evokes turf protection when no highly effective collaboration exists. Hence, affirmative action programs work best when handled by a top management task force working in conjunction with an Equal Employment Opportunity (EEO) staff member. Without the management group, this staff member can only cajole, theaten, and beg to persuade managers to do their part.

Affirmative action covers all personnel management functions, including hiring, recruitment, training, firing, and awards. Organizations must assess and alter management practices in all of these areas to remove discriminatory practices. As Diane Herrmann, the Director of Office of Equal Opportunity Programs at the Department of the Treasury, told me recently,

It is critical each year to analyze and target priorities and to focus resources. We are talking about changes in manage-

ment practices that will take years. Each year we work at moving toward parity. One year the priority may be shortening the time frame from the current two to three years it may take to process discrimination complaints in the federal government. The next year, it may be emphasizing training which could include an upward mobility program, awareness training for managers and information on sexual harassment.

The following issues are central to developing a total systems affirmative action program:

• To what extent does the organization now value management of human resources?

• What is the current organizational culture for women, minorities, and white males? What would improve the climate for the employees and the organization?

• What sort of management resources does the organization need to make affirmative action work in recruiting, hiring, training, mentoring, monitoring the progress of women and minorities, and increasing the effectiveness of supervisors?

To deal with these questions, organizations need a total systems change model for affirmative action. I developed this approach when I worked for over four years with a large manufacturing company and have used segments of it in government agencies and several other manufacturing companies (see Figure 1).

The model for total systems change

1. The best situation occurs when the organization appoints a *top management task force* to set goals and objectives for affirmative action, to develop a plan, and to ensure enforcement. Provide this team with the following: data on employee utilization; and workforce analysis by gender, race, and job classification to determine status of women and minorities; an availability study for each job group; and statistical information on selection, training programs attended, and promotion.

2. Conduct a *climate survey* to collect data on the quality of work life for women and minorities. Use group-sensing

sessions to collect data so that group discussions occur in both homogeneous and heterogeneous groups.

3. Design an effective *recruiting and hiring* program that employs women and minority recruiters. Identify areas of underuse and analyze barriers.

4. Assess *management systems* for their effectiveness in the affirmative action effort, particularly the performance appraisal process that monitors equal employment opportunity and the career development system.

5. Provide *training* programs that include women and minority managers. Offer supervisor/woman manager pairs training, supervisor/minority manager pairs training, and supervisor/secretary workshops. Mandate team building for groups that include women and minorities. Conduct awareness sessions on racism, sexism, and antidiscrimination. Include training modules in ongoing management education programs.

6. Promote *supervisory* relationships that fulfill such

human resource management functions as managerial coaching, career development, performance management, and development of high-potential but poor-performing employees.

7. Assess *upward-mobility* programs to evaluate the effectiveness of placement and targeting for jobs.

8. Provide such *alternative work schedules* arrangements as flexitime, job sharing, part-time work, and child care.

9. Encourage *network building* among women and minorities, such as minority managers' work groups.

10. Establish a *spouse-involvement program* to explain affirmative action and to deal with such issues as health benefits, financial planning, and men and women working and traveling together.

11. Create *affirmative action teams* to identify problems and carry out programs.

Figure 1
Steps in a Total Systems Affirmative Action Program

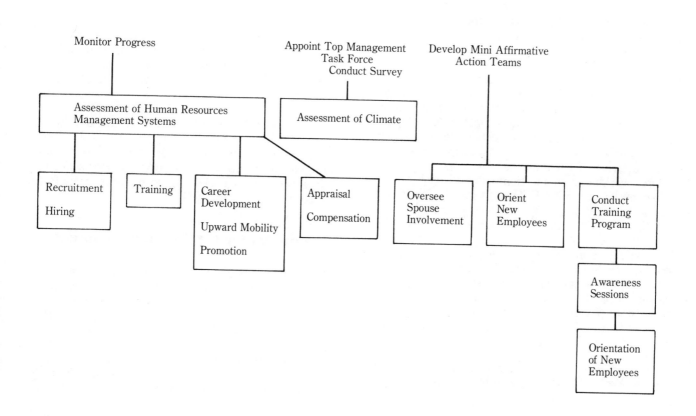

1. Top management task force

The task force needs a key decision maker who can assure organizational commitment to affirmative action efforts. Neither personnel nor the Equal Employment Opportunity office should direct the task force, but they should help staff it. The task force's basic goals are to change the climate, structures, policies, practices, and interpersonal relationships within the organization to eliminate discrimination and to build a multicultural work environment.

Affirmative action task forces commonly begin work with off-site team building. For several days, team members work with external resources to increase their awareness of the issues and to build a better understanding among themselves. In one instance, an all-male task force recognized that they could not commit themselves to the effort until they discovered their own reasons for joining the affirmative action group. These men were asked to list 10 ways affirmative action would benefit them. For several men, the only obvious answer was that their helping promote women and minorities provided one measure of managerial effectiveness on their performance appraisal. Several managers wanted to understand the issues because women in their families had become deeply involved in consciousness-raising groups or had returned to work or to school. No one could suggest more than two reasons.

A reading list helped task-force members learn about issues and, particularly, to identify male sex-role expectations. Some men in manufacturing doubted that women could perform the required physical work. The men had a lingering concern that women possessed less strength and energy. Therefore, task-force members talked about the implications of such sex-linked characteristics as the physiological effects of testosterone and estrogen. The men thought that physical education programs and sex-role stereotypes in the educational system helped perpetuate the physical differences between the sexes. The most compelling logic presented was that the bona fide occupational requirement in most states for lifting ranges from 35-50 pounds; women routinely lift children or grocery bags that exceed 35 pounds.

The task force developed an action plan that established affirmative action goals for the next several years. The goal included the following: data collection on the climate for women and minorities; recruitment, with women helping recruit for the first time; hiring objectives; and an upward-mobility program that considered educational backgrounds other than engineering. The task force also planned training, supervisor/secretary workshops, family awareness groups in the plant, work groups for women managers, and "mini" affirmative action teams composed of male-female pairs and minority-white pairs for each manufacturing module that comprised aproximately 75 employees.

2. Climate survey

A team of women and men should interview white women and male managers and minority women and men—both individually and in groups—to identify the factors that contribute to an effective or ineffective work climate for women and minorities. A paper-and-pencil questionnaire does not help nearly as much as an interview, for it usually measures only the level of awareness, not the nature of the climate.

3. Recruitment programs

When recruiting women and minorities, a central need is the identification of new networks and new contact persons. Networks that can lead organizations to minorities and to women exist in all areas. Organizations must also build credible relationships with women and minority faculty in universities who can refer their students to employers. These approaches suggest the depth and significance of affirmative action. It frequently requires a sizeable change in organizational attitudes and practices, because organizations generally lack the institutional mechanisms to draw on these resources and to radically shift old hiring patterns. If business continues to function the way it always has, it will not yield new patterns. Adopting affirmative action requires major restructuring.

4. Assess management systems: Performance appraisal

Performance appraisal is the critical management system for effecting the changes sought in an affirmative action effort. If organizations do not evaluate and reward or punish managers for their behavior in implementing affirmative action, the system will lack accountability. Therefore, each manager must have a management by objectives (MBO) plan that emphasizes clear performance criteria for hiring, developing, promoting, and supervising women and minorities. Craig Schneier, professor of personnel and organizational behavior at the University of Maryland, told me (in 1976),

> In order to implement an effective affirmative action program, a manager's effort must be anchored to the reward system. The evaluation tool for this performance appraisal system makes explicit the degree to which the manager's behavior is responsive to the affirmative action plan.

5. Training programs

Few white male managers have had much contact with women or minority professionals. Awareness workshops that address such issues as dealing with differences, style versus competence, dependency, control, and sexuality can help these managers. Furthermore, coalitions or support systems between women and minorities can increase these persons' awareness, skill, and effectiveness in communicating their feelings.

People in organizations have only begun to learn to work with a heterogeneous population; their social lives, however, have experienced little integration at all. Awareness provides the first step toward collaborative behavior across racial and gender differences. People do not yet understand differences in style, dress, language patterns, topics of conversations, and laughter—and this lack of familiarity keeps them apart.

Issues to be covered in awareness workshops

Competence. Since competent men and women may not have the same styles, they must be able to differentiate between style and competence. Significant gender differences occur in verbal and non-verbal behavior, namely in the areas of touch, interpersonal space, gaze, and body movement (Mayo & Henley, 1981). All of these elements have power and warmth and dimensions, but people interpret them differently, depending upon whether they are displayed by women or by men. Studies document that women can more skillfully decode non-verbal cues than men can. Therefore, since women are more partner-oriented, non-verbal behavior more likely affects women's responses than those of men. Eileen Morley (1976) of the Harvard Business School has pointed out that women tend to feel/think and men tend to think/feel. In other words, when you ask a woman what she is thinking, she may report her feelings; when you ask a man what he is feeling, he may report his thoughts. In a world dominated by male values, managers need to be able to recognize competent behavior in different styles.

Dependency. Under present practices of socialization, dependency typically is encouraged in girls and discouraged in boys. This has led to what has been labelled the "Cinderella Complex" in women and to "learned helplessness" in both genders when they face certain tasks. Men may experience learned helplessness in the work place, for example, when they must get coffee or deal with tears, whereas women may experience it when dealing with numbers and statistics. In terms used in transactional analysis, this leads to parent-child inter-actions rather than adult-adult behavior. Some examples of the types of communication follow.

• *Father-son.* Rather than acknowledge vulnerability, male managers adopt a can-do approach until they make themselves physically sick.

• *Mother-boy.* Men use women managers as mothers by telling them personal information instead of treating them as real colleagues with whom they also solve problems and perform tasks.

• *Father-girl.* Male managers become angry at women employees but also protect them.

• *Mother-boy.* Male managers defer to female managers in emotional situations in which pain is being expressed. The woman comforts an employee who cries, while the man steps aside.

• *Father-girl.* Women managers defer to male managers during policy making or budget appropriations.

Control. Men are used to being in control in mixed groups and women are not. Habitual patterns of respond-ing to control become critical when men and women managers work together—and when women manage men.

To achieve communication among equals in work interactions, managers must eliminate the following behaviors:

• *Girl-girl or mother-girl.* Women managers fail to share their competence with one another.

• *Father-girl and mother-boy.* Men and women managers use sex for power and control.

A parent-child interaction may feel more comfortable because it is familiar and because it helps people deny that sexual attraction exists. Managers must explore these dimensions in awareness programs and use skill building to re-educate both men and women so that they can interact as adults.

Sexuality. Both actual incidents of sexual relationships that develop through work and fantasies and anxieties about it make sexuality a more pervasive issue in the work place than many anticipated. Sexuality always exists in male-female interactions, whether it takes the form of attraction or discounting. Rarely, indeed, do men and women not appraise one another sexually.

Without discussion, men and women may not under-stand why they are attracted to one another. Their fantasies may escalate, and they may feel that the pressure of feelings denies them a sense of choice. Yet we know that the reasons for this attraction may include curiosity, the desire for power or control, boredom, joy, and love. Talking about their motivation may defuse fantasies—or at least clarify the terms of the relationship. When people feel attracted to one another sexually in a way that interferes with work, the situation must be discussed for the sake of the people involved and of the organization.

Differentiated competency based training modules

Sex-role stereotyping and differential socialization have caused some men and women to acquire different abilities. Business, government, and academe have valued masculine competence highly. Men and women, therefore, need training to recognize each other's skills, and organizations need to learn to value the "feminine" skills that men can learn to benefit from. We describe men and women who display skills associated with both masculine and feminine styles as *androgynous*.

To be androgynous, some women may need to learn to do the following:

• be powerful and forthright and have a direct, visible impact on others rather than function behind the scenes;

• initiate and take risks, despite their visibility and vulnerability;

• state their own needs and not back down, even if these needs are not immediately accepted;

• focus on a task and regard it as at least as important as the relationships of the people performing it;

• build support systems with other women and share knowledge with women rather than competing with them;

• analyze and generalize from experience;

• behave "impersonally" more often rather than always personalizing experiences;

• stop turning anger, blame, and pain inward, which causes them to reject feelings of suffering and victimization;

• reject feedback when it is inappropriate;

• respond directly with "I" statements rather than with blaming "you" statements;

• become effective problem solvers who are analytical, systematic, and directive rather than fearful or dependent; and

• stop such self-limiting behaviors as allowing oneself to be interrupted or laughing after making a serious statement.

To be androgynous, some men may need to learn to do the following:

• become aware of feelings rather than avoiding or suppressing them;

• regard feelings as basic and essential to life, rather than as impediments to achievement;

• accept a share of responsibility for "providing," but refuse total responsibility;

• assert the right to work for self-fulfillment rather than as mere "providers";

• value an identity that is not defined totally by work;

• learn to accept failure at tasks without feeling they have failed as men;

• accept and express the need to be nurtured when feeling hurt, afraid, vulnerable, or helpless, rather than hiding those feelings behind a mask of strength and rationality;

• be close to both men and women;

• listen actively and be empathic without feeling responsible for problem solving;

• build support systems and friendships with other men, sharing competence without competition;

• personalize experience, rather than assuming that the only valid approach to life and interpersonal contact is "objective";

• accept the emotional, spontaneous, and irrational as valid parts of themselves to be explored and expressed as needed and to openly express their feelings of love, anger, pain, joy, loneliness, and dependency;

• understand how men value women as "validators of masculinity," havens from the competitive male world, the expressive partners;

• understand the impact that being male has on shaping their lives and their responses; and

• nurture and actively support men and women in their efforts to change (Sargent, 1977).

6. Supervisory relationships

The most critical component for women's and minorities' success is their relationships with their supervisors. This comes as no surprise given what we know about the importance of "expectation effects" in teacher-pupil relationships and intimate relationships. Expectation effects critically affect success or failure on the job, in school, and in marriage. As Robert Rosenthal (1969) reported on IQ scores, the children who received higher numbers—although the scores were false—improved more quickly because of teacher expectations. The so-called "bright" rats learned mazes more quickly because of researcher expectations. Behavioral scientists regard the supervisory relationship as a major factor in women's or minorities' success.

Research on personnel interviewers by Rosen and Jerdee (1974) underscores how interview bias can determine whether women or men enter a system. Furthermore, supervisors may hold the same stereotypes as the interviewers. For example, interviewers in industry expect men to be effective because they believe men understand financial matters, analyze situations, like science and math, know how to set long-range goals, and want to get ahead. Characteristics attributed to women include enjoyment of routine, sensitivity to criticism, timidity, jealousy, overemotionalism, sensitivity to the feelings of others, a tendency to quit more frequently than men, and a propensity to put family matters ahead of the job. In fact, women do not have more job instability than men, and they do not necessarily enjoy routine more than men. Managers who hold such stereotypes generally act upon them. Male supervisors report that they feel more sympathetic when home life interferes with a man's work. The manager helps male employees by suggesting such solutions to the problem as different kinds of services or counseling. The supervisor probably thinks, "After all, he's the primary breadwinner." But supervisors commonly hold an "I knew it was going to happen" attitude when a woman's home life interferes with her work.

To illustrate the sex-linked differences in expectations of supervisors, Kathryn Bartol and Anthony Butterfield (1976) reversed the names of men and women in a number of case studies. They found sex-linked differences regarding assumed effectiveness on two components of managerial behavior: (a) initiating structure (considered masculine) and (b) showing concern for others (considered feminine). In the initiating structure exercise (a), participants were asked to rate managers for effectiveness based on the three weeks they spent in a new office finding out what was happening and then developing a reorganization plan. Only the names of the managers were changed; the behaviors remained the same. The participants rated the men as more effective than the women, whom they described as autocratic, taking too much initiative, and undemocratic. Sexual prejudice cuts both ways. In contrast, regarding concern for others (b), the participants rated the women managers as effective when they sought the opinions and feelings of others and became involved with employees who had problems. But participants described a male manager who used the same approach as wishy-washy and as becoming overly involved.

The solution is not for men to give up their proactive organizing style or for women to become directive at the expense of feelings and concern for others. Both sexes would enhance their effectiveness by learning the attitudes and behaviors generally attributed to the other sex and by developing a blend. Compensatory training can help both men and women develop qualities of so-called "masculine" independence and "feminine"

nurturance.

Similar issues exist in building a multicultural environment across races. The values learned from the experience could also change the nature of the organizational life. The majority group of white people subconsciously develops an arrogance that could be tempered by humility. White people also tend to rely too much on rationality—which could be mediated by the "common sense," more natural approach of many minorities.

7. Upward mobility programs: Career development

When management seeks the effective promotion of women and minorities, it will find unclear career paths and a lack of long-range human resource planning. For effectiveness and for morale to improve, all employees must have a sense of where they are going in the organization and what it takes to get there. This comes from specific information about career paths, targeted jobs, and developmental assignments that lead to specifc positions.

8. Alternative work schedules

While women have widely supported alternative work opportunities, men now find them valuable, too. The specific alternative work schedules that organizations have tried and found successful include flexible working hours, the compressed work week, permanent part-time work, and job sharing. The organization benefits from these options through increased productivity; higher morale; retaining highly competent employees who only want part-time work because of other demands in their lives; reduced absenteeism, tardiness, and turnover; and a progressive image that may attract other employees. Individuals benefit from the opportunity to be at home when children arrive from school; the opportunity for two-career couples to share child care; more leisure time for education, home life, and developing other sides of one's identity; commuting at different hours; the opportunity to work during the hours of the day when one feels most effective; and opportunities for additional work.

9. Coalition building among women and minorities

Networks for women and minority managers help both new and old employees. Such groups also help the organization to recruit, orient, and retain employees. Groups of minority or women managers can identify key concerns, ranging from promotion to maternity leave to part-time work.

Over a period of time, coalitions can alter the typical pattern of entry into the system for minorities and women. New female employees often try to succeed in the white male-dominated workplace without first turning to other women or minorities for friendship and support. In this process of proving themselves, many women take on necessary so-called "masculine" characteristics when dealing with power and conflict and shed some of their valuable "feminine" behavior of nurturance and spontaneity. This causes them to suffer a great deal from a sense of frustration and failure.

Many women report that they avoid being branded as too seductive or nurturing by reducing their emotional responses when they are the only women in a group. One corporate affirmative action program dealt with the problem of the lone woman by focusing on a natural work group—such as a mechanical engineering department. When a woman prepared to join the group, members talked about the issues involved both before and after she joined. The group held follow-up sessions because instances of isolation developed quite quickly even when they were temporarily solved. She just wasn't "one of the boys" and thus part of the informal communication network.

Women's networks offer an important way to deal with the problems of isolation, loneliness, and pressure to conform to male norms. They provide a sanctuary where women can express feelings of frustration, anger, or loneliness in a concerned environment. Because they participated in these coalitions, a number of women indicated that they felt better able to hold on to their own style and sense of self-worth rather than merely adopting the dominant male patterns.

Affirmative action efforts highlight tension and the lack of communication between women and minorities. Often, style differences create barriers. Sometimes black men and white women fear that they will be used by each other. The relationship becomes complicated by fantasies about power and sexual attraction. Women think black men can have power because they are men; black men think white women have access to power by asking their men for it. Both groups would benefit from joining forces and acknowledging that neither group has had much access to information or power.

10. Spouse involvement

Organizations often like to keep the personal lives of their employees quite separate from their work lives, but women's entrance into the workforce necessarily combines the two. The greatest concern develops when men and women travel together on business trips and experience more relaxed norms and opportunities for closer contact. Instead of pretending that sexual attraction and sexual harassment could never arise, organizations that have dealt directly with such issues have been able to defuse some of the fantasies and problems. Spouse involvement in affirmative action programs has altered the traditional split between work and home life and has improved morale and cooperation. In affirmative action programs, spouses have also discussed mobility policy, which can help them prepare for a move. Other significant topics include child-care policies, cafeteria benefits, flexitime for two-career couples, and health benefits.

11. Affirmative action teams

One organization established male-female and black-white pairs for each department. The teams informed new employees about affirmative action activities. The teams also identified the development of occupational stereotyping by noting what became women's work in the plant. For example, quality control jobs quickly became women's work. The teams also monitored the progress of women and minorities and served as troubleshooters.

When possible, each team included the technical training director. In a manufacturing environment, one training director obtained additional technical training for women. The program was so successful that men also sought the training. Affirmative action provided everyone with an opportunity to improve themselves and altered ineffective management training practices.

Summary

In the total systems approach, affirmative action becomes a management problem. The organization views women and minorities as the experts who can solve this problem with important assistance from the human resources office. The goal is for key decision makers to take on the problem and to use their analytical and interpersonal competence to solve it. All decision makers become involved so that no one feels her or his territory has been invaded.

Social and psychological research indicates that behavior changes precede attitude changes. Action may elicit a different kind of response from the habitual one. Changes in the reward system can produce further changes in both behavior and attitudes. The first phase of change is to increase awareness of and responsibility for problems. Organizations maintain momentum through such incentives as performance appraisal, coalitions among women and minorities, and temporary structures within the system—e.g., a mini affirmative action team. Organizations need at least three to five years to produce initial changes.

This approach benefits the white male who now holds power in the organization by increasing his life options and his work options. It also helps women and minorities who seek equal power and influence in the workplace. The total systems approach offers people the chance to change organizational patterns of majority dominance and minority dependence and frustration.

A reallocation of power and influence occurs along with the development of new networks across more heterogeneous segments of the American population. A shifting of the organizational norms to encompass members of the new workforce also occurs. America appears to be experiencing a value shift: The U.S. is no longer a melting pot, but is actually developing a multicultural environment.

References

Bartol, K. M., & Butterfield, D. Sex effects in evaluating leaders. *Journal of Applied Psychology*, 1976, *61*(4).

Mayo, C., & Henley, N. M. *Gender and nonverbal behavior*. New York: Springer-Verlag, 1981.

Morley, E. Women's thinking and talking. *Harvard Business School, Case No. 9-477-055*. Boston Mass.: Harvard Case Clearing House, 1976.

Rosen, B., & Jerdee, T. H. Effects of applicant's sex and difficulty of job on evaluations of candidates for managerial positions. *Journal of Applied Psychology*, 1974, *59*(4), 511.

Rosenthal, R., & Jacobson, L. *Pygmalion in the classroom*. New York: Holt, Rinehart & Winston, 1969.

Sargent, A. G. *Beyond sex roles*. St. Paul, Minn.: West Publishing, 1977.

For further reading

Aries, E. Male-female interpersonal styles in all-male, all-female and mixed groups. In A. G. Sargent (Ed.), *Beyond sex roles*. St. Paul, Minn.: West Publishing, 1977.

Bartolome, F., & Evans, P. A. L. Must success cost so much? *Harvard Business Review*, March-April 1980.

Jackson, B., & Hardiman, R. Racial identity development: Implications for managing the multiracial work force. *The NTL managers' handbook*. Arlington, Va.: NTL Institute, 1983.

Leavitt, H. J., & Lipman-Blumen. A case for the relational manager. *Organizational Dynamics*, 1980, 27-41.

Sargent, A. G. *The androgynous manager*. New York: AMACOM, 1981.

Wilkins, R. *A Man's life: An autobiography*. New York: Simon & Schuster, 1982.

Some Learnings from a Third-Party Assisted Joint Union-Management Project

JOHN J. SHERWOOD, STEPHEN L. McCLURE,
AND DONALD C. KING

A corporate management group from a large multi-national manufacturing company, which we will refer to as Midwest Manufacturing (MM), contacted the first and third authors to explore the possibility of their providing consulting assistance. The issues were to understand better and to ameliorate a long-developing crisis in the relationship between the management of one of Midwest Manufacturing's plants, particularly the Middleton plant, and the local union. This paper describes significant events from a four-year consultation *vis a vis* the involvement of the consultants, some noteworthy outcomes, and the significant learnings that resulted. We also include ideas of other authors involved in joint union-management organizational change efforts. The result is a chronological progression through issues which surfaced in the consultation with discussions of choices available to consultants.

Adoption of a joint union-management (JUM) project

Traditionally, management takes responsibility for contacting a consultant rather than a union (Beer & Driscoll, 1977), and in the case of Midwest Manufacturing (MM), corporate management took initiative for arranging the initial discussion with the consultants. The consultants were then faced with a situation in which they had had a conversation with corporate management, but in which neither the local plant management nor the local union were at this point involved. Therefore, the first step was to assess interest and obtain commitment from both union and management at the local level, and then to clarify relationships between the consultants, the corporation, the local union, and the local plant management.

The contract and resistance to change

The consultants made clear in the initial project proposal their preference for a contract with the local parties and

one which specified that the local union was an equal partner with local management. The client was carefully defined as the union *and* management at the Middleton MM plant. An explicit statement to include the union as an equal partner was necessary because a meaningful understanding of the relationship was not thought possible without the active support of the local union.

Once the proposal was accepted by corporate management, the consultants needed to consider how to enter the organization at the Middleton plant level. Management will often resist sharing control of an intervention with a union and, likewise, cooperating with management is a risky step for union leadership. Joint union-management (JUM) programs nearly always require shared power between union and management, and managers often experience codetermination as a loss of power and prerogatives. In addition, union leaders are sensitive to negative reactions they anticipate from their constituencies in response to their visible collaboration with management. Between the two groups it is probably the union that offers the greater challenge in getting a JUM project started. While some forces facilitate acceptance, many factors encouraging resistance often are stronger (Drexler & Lawler, 1977).

To the extent that changes—or proposed changes—that accompany a JUM project challenge management's or the union's values, powers, images, objectives, and influence, the project will be resisted; and to the extent that changes appear to further desired outcomes, the project will be supported (Beer & Driscoll, 1977). Therefore, the acceptance of a JUM project will be in part a function of the perceptions by key union and management personnel as to whether or not the project will lead to valued outcomes (Kochan & Dyer, 1976). Thus, it is in the interest of getting a proposal accepted that valued goals of both groups are emphasized by consultants. In this way both groups are in better positions to make informed choices.

Initial contact: The issue of consultant bias

Given that management usually makes the initial contact with the consultant, one should expect that consultants will have to overcome what the union may understandably perceive as a management bias. This was anticipated in the MM case and was successfully managed by the consultants during their initial contact with the union. When the consultants first met with union officers, the consultants themselves suggested three questions that the union would have about the consultants: (1) Are these consultants competent in union-management relations? (2) Are these third parties unbiased with respect to unions? and (3) Are these outsiders naive and being used by management? The union leadership was receptive to a discussion with the two consultants organized regarding these questions. After a give-and-take discussion, the union officials believed they had enough information to answer these questions. Later, however, a different problem with bias emerged.

After the union decided to become involved in the project, the consultants actively tried to reduce any perception of management bias by taking precautions to see union representatives first and also last during every plant visit. While they succeeded with the union in this respect, their cautious behavior elicited suspicion among some middle managers who perceived the consultants as having a union bias. The solution which evolved was that management began to identify more strongly with one consultant and the union with the other; each consultant became a contact for one party. This development was not discouraged by the consultants.

During their first visit to the MM plant, the consultants requested that arrangements be made for them to meet jointly with both local plant management and union representatives. As it turned out, the consultants met only with top management during their initial visit; and in retrospect, the consultants now believe it was naive on their part to expect management to arrange a joint meeting without the consultants having secured prior and independent approval of themselves as third parties by both union and management. If union-management relations were such that they could sit down together and talk about joint ventures, they probably would not require the assistance of third parties to help them examine their relationship.

Largely because MM corporate management had a clear interest in a JUM project at Middleton, local management accepted the proposal to work jointly with the union and with the consultants. In doing so, plant management probably saw themselves as responding principally to the expectations of corporate and division management.

Interventions

Following an initial meeting with the union bargaining committee, the union decided to go along with the proposal that emphasized data collection by interviewing key union members and managers followed by feedback and action planning. The interviews were completed and data analyzed, and after reporting the results of the interviews, an action plan was discussed with both parties. The consultants then prepared a proposal for a jointly sponsored

and managed project that would address important problems affecting both management and union, such as absenteeism and maintenance of equipment. It was expected that through joint problem solving relations between the two parties would be clarified and improved. The union promptly rejected the proposal, and once again the consultants were faced with gaining union acceptance.

After a union election, a new chairman of the shop committee came into office. He had considered a career as a union official beyond the bounds of the Middleton plant. He saw the JUM project as a vehicle for attracting the attention of the international union, particularly since joint union-management ventures to improve the quality of work life were being given high priority and visibility by the international union. The election of a new local union official proved to be instrumental in regaining the union's support and renewed interest in a JUM project.

Support for a strategy of gaining acceptance of a JUM project by using existing influence structures is found in a model of entry developed by the Institute for Social Research together with the National Quality of Work Life Center. A "multi-tier structure" is used for the introduction of quality-of-work-life programs that involves the formation of multiple levels of JUM committees beginning at the highest level in both organizations (Drexler & Lawler, 1977). Once formed, each committee is then responsible for the formation of the next tier below it and so on down to the level at which changes are to be made. Such an approach uses the hierarchical power structures that exist in both organizations. While the technique may have many variations, a top-down approach is useful to overcome barriers to change which appear minor when compared to the immediate consequences of not complying with the interests of one's superior in the hierarchy.

JUM projects and collective bargaining

Another lesson that resulted from working with the union at MM was the need for the consultants to make clear their commitment to the preservation of the jurisdiction of the collective-bargaining mechanism. All parties agreed that the proposed JUM project was at all times to be outside and separate from the formal and traditional collective-bargaining arrangements (Kochan & Dyer, 1976; Drexler & Lawler, 1977). It is important that the JUM project remain auxilliary and independent of collective bargaining because collective bargaining brought the union to power, and any threat to collective bargaining is a threat to the union's security as an organization. In addition, collective bargaining is an appropriate way of resolving differences when there is competition for scarce resources (Walton & McKersie, 1965). Such fears are best addressed if they are anticipated and care is taken to clarify the distinction between a collaborative JUM project and the competition of collective bargaining. While improvements in the overall relationship—with positive spillover into collective bargaining—were expected, the JUM concept is no replacement for formal collective bargaining.

Consultant activities and JUM committee processes

As previously mentioned, local plant management viewed their initial involvement as compliance with the expectations of corporate management. In contrast, the local union was initially completely on its own to decide whether they would become involved and appeared to do so because they viewed involvement as a low-cost investment with the possibility for some gains. Such gains could either embarrass local management or provide an opportunity to build credit by cooperating on a question important to local management but of lesser importance to the union. While the project was conceived with the purpose of developing better labor-management relations, it was clear that each party initially viewed the project as a potential source from which they might gain—or in the case of local management, might avoid loss or negative sanctions from the corporate hierarchy. Such a view was entirely consistent with their history of conflict and crisis negotiations.

The JUM committee

The original mixed-motive nature of the JUM committee made problem solving nearly impossible since each party focused exclusively on self-interest, whereas the objectives of collaborative problem solving are outcomes with advantages to both parties. The consultants had to recognize that each party was responding in its own self-interests and to accept such behavior as legitimate and historically necessary. Just because each party knows the JUM project's goals and each agrees to participate, consultants cannot naively assume an immediate shift to open collaboration. Similarly, it is necessary to recognize existing power and political ties in each organization both internal and external to the JUM committee. Effective consultants cannot behave as if power and politics do not exist (Harrison, 1970).

The approach taken by the consultants with the MM plant was to assist in the development of the JUM committee as a single entity which nevertheless contained representatives of two groups that had realistically adversarial traditions outside of the JUM efforts. They then provided the joint group and others throughout the plant with a means of referring to and addressing the newly formed JUM committee. The consultants recognized the JUM committee as one group in which both agreement and disagreement existed. Confrontation and support were evenly divided between the two parties, and when confrontation and support were given, individuals were the recipients rather than union or management. The only time support was given to more than one person was

when it was extended to the entire committee, thus creating opportunities for the JUM committee to identify itself as a unit.

The consultant role

One result of the long-standing adversarial relationship between union and management at this plan was the JUM committee's initial inability to accomplish anything that required much cooperation. At first, they could not even agree on a place or a time to meet, and when they did get together they both approached most matters as issues to be bargained over rather than as problems to be solved. The consultants learned that they could not rely on the parties to prepare minutes of meetings without the consultants overseeing their efforts. The consultants also found that if they did not provide the structure and gain explicit commitment on every detail, such minor tasks were never accomplished. Similarly, the consultants had to structure the exchange in JUM meetings so that agreement or disagreement was reached on each point; they could not assume that silence on the part of any individual meant agreement. The consultants, therefore, provided a high level of structure and initiative which the JUM committee required during its initial stages but which the parties themselves were unable to provide.

Support for a directive approach in establishing JUM committees is offered by Brown (1973) and Nadler (1978a and b), who argue that in intense conflict situations, where union-management relations are very poor, a highly directive intervention strategy is most successful. A directive approach was required initially by the consultants at MM, but their ultimate goal was to adopt the role of process consultants thereby developing commitment and ownership of the project within the JUM committee. At Midwest Manufacturing a move from directive to process roles on the part of the consultants was accomplished, in part, by their refusal to do tasks which the parties were legitimately in better positions to do. For example, such tasks as preparing written documents—reports or minutes—were better suited to the parties themselves because they were in much better positions to provide wording which was consistent with their contract, history, or protocol. The consultants provided the structure for task accomplishment, but the actual tasks were performed by the JUM committee in progressive steps from those which required little collaboration to those which required much more collaboration. In addition, the consultants regularly provided concepts, models, and practice opportunities to the JUM committee on problem-solving skills which, combined with the parties' greater involvement in joint tasks, resulted in both parties gaining confidence with self-direction and their own responsibilities for the effectiveness of the project. The result was a slow, and mixed, transition from distributive bargaining behaviors (Walton & McKersie, 1965) to more integrative and collaborative problem-solving behaviors from both parties. A longitudinal view of the process would demonstrate a gradual decrease in directiveness and an increase in process interventions on the part of the consultants. It was not a smooth transition, however, because the emergence of special issues and the influence of problematic events outside JUM committee jurisdiction often required a reversal to a directive posture by the consultants.

The JUM project

While the history of the JUM committee resulted in increasingly more collaborative actions and expressed attitudes, the content of the JUM committee's discussions narrowed the list of alternatives for joint projects. The final two alternatives were the maintenance of production equipment and absenteeism. Equipment maintenance was of considerable concern to the union because they did not want their members working with poorly maintained and potentially dangerous equipment; whereas management was concerned with productivity losses resulting from equipment breakdown. Absenteeism concerned union officials because chronic offenders left their workmates to fill in while they were absent, and absenteeism also depleted the union's resources in the grievance mechanism. Management was concerned with the loss of both productivity and quality. The JUM committee selected an absenteeism project primarily because it was not clear how union officials might contribute to improving equipment maintenance. The committee believed that both union and management could contribute equally to the absenteeism problem, and any gains from their efforts were perceived as being roughly equivalent. Another reason for choosing absenteeism as their initial collaborative project was because the MM plant's manufacturing facilities were, at that time, being heavily taxed because of high production demands, and a joint project focusing on poorly maintained equipment would have been very difficult to implement. Therefore, the first JUM project chosen was to design and implement a system of joint counseling of chronically absent employees by the union committeeman and foreman within a section of the plant.

One of the most important contributions a consultant makes in a newly formed JUM committee is to provide necessary guidance for selection of an appropriate first project. The choice of an initial project is obviously important because it is a test to both parties of the JUM concept. In addition, the first step is a risky one for both parties, and if they can achieve small and early successes, they will begin to develop both the trust and confidence necessary to take larger risks with greater potential joint pay-offs.

What makes the first project so critical is that both parties are under close scrutiny by their constituencies, especially by the cynics and skeptics among them, and if either side feels burned—whether true or not—by their

involvement this will sour them toward any future collaborative endeavors. Both sides have low involvement in the early stages of JUM committee functioning, and, therefore, low commitment. Given the fragile nature of the committee, it is wise to spend considerable effort developing the best project available. An optimal first project has potential for payoff in the perceptions of both the union and management in roughly equal amounts along both quality and quantity dimensions. In general, criteria for selection of a first project are as follows. The project should

1. be experienced as real and important by both parties;
2. be viewed as one in which improvement is possible;
3. not be seen as exclusively a problem for one party or for some third party;
4. be a problem toward which both parties agree that each can and should contribute to its resolution;
5. be one which both parties agree that each stands to gain by addressing the problem jointly.

The first and second criteria need elaboration because they are more complex than they appear to be. The scope of the initial project should be limited for several reasons. The less dependent the success of the project is on others, the more control the JUM committee has; second, it is within the JUM committee that commitment to successful collaboration is the highest. Furthermore, a shorter time frame for project completion means rewards will be felt sooner, which in turn serve to support the risks taken by JUM committee members. Kochan and Dyer (1976), Nadler (1978a and b), and Beer and Driscoll (1977) all agree that initial projects need to be limited in scope for greater potential success. Also, the first issue should not be difficult or complex, but perhaps more importantly, it should not be of such little significance that sufficient interest does not exist and little risk is involved. While subsequent problems should also be chosen with care, the initial project is a pilot during which new skills are developed and the relationship between union and management members is expanded to include collaborative attitudes and behaviors. The initial project also serves as a demonstration project to those intimately involved as well as to observers from various constituencies.

Conclusion

The project at the MM plant came to an end approximately four years after its initiation because of the lack of support from a new plant manager (the third plant manager during the life of the project). As with most organizational interventions, if support does not exist within the formal power structure, the commitment necessary for success is lost. Following the absenteeism project, however, individuals involved in formal contract negotiations believed that they had gone better than at any time in memory. Both sides were more willing to address themselves to the real issues separating them and the customary futile pursuit of unimportant concerns by both parties was much less prevalent during local negotiations. Also, both sides saw themselves as better organized internally and were therefore better prepared to deliver the facts about negotiated issues. While the absenteeism project resulted in only a slight reduction in absenteeism, there was spillover into other parts of the working relationship between union and management at the MM plant.

Nadler (1978a and b) collected data from managers, union officials, and active rank and file organization members where JUM projects were taking place or had recently taken place. The results indicate that the consultant's effectiveness is more important to successful outcomes in JUM projects than participant ownership of the project, goal clarity or consensus, effectiveness of JUM committee functioning, or the level of trust among members. Specifically, consultant behavior such as ability to "make things happen," resolve conflict, facilitate communication, and facilitate intergroup functioning were judged to be most closely related to success. In general, active leadership was found to be the greatest strength of consultants, and poor leadership and misunderstanding of the system were found to be the greatest weaknesses.

References

Beer, M., & Driscoll, J. W. Strategies for change. In J. R. Hackman & J. L. Suttle (Eds.), *Improving life at work: Behavior sciences approaches to organizational change.* Santa Monica, Calif.: Goodyear Press, 1977.

Brown, B. R. Reflections on missing the broadside of a barn. *The Journal of Applied Behavioral Science*, 1973, *9*(4), 450-458.

Drexler, J. A., Jr., & Lawler, E. E. III. A union-management cooperative project to improve the quality of work life. *The Journal of Applied Behavioral Science*, 1977, *13*(3), 373-387.

Harrison, R. Choosing the depth of organizational intervention. *The Journal of Applied Behavioral Science*, 1970, *6*(2), 181-202.

Kochan, T. A., & Dyer, L. A model of organizational change in the context of union-management relations. *The Journal of Applied Behavioral Science*, 1976, *12*(1), 59-78.

Nadler, D. A. Hospitals, organized labor and quality of work: An intervention case study. *The Journal of Applied Behavioral Science*, 1978, *14*(3), 366-381 (a).

Nadler, D. A. Consulting with labor and management: Some learnings from quality of working life projects. In W. W. Burke (Ed.), *The cutting edge: Current concepts and strategies in organizational development.* La Jolla, Calif.: University Associates, 1978 (b).

Walton, R. E., & McKersie, R. B. *A behavioral theory of labor negotiations: An analysis of a social interaction system.* New York: McGraw-Hill, 1965.

For Further Reading

Argyris, Chris. *Interpersonal Competence and Organizational Effectiveness.* Homewood, Ill.: Richard D. Irwin, 1962.

Argyris, Chris. *Organization and Innovation.* Homewood, Ill.: Richard D. Irwin, 1965.

Beckhard, Richard. *Organization Development: Developing Strategies and Models.* Reading, Mass.: Addison-Wesley, 1969.

Benne, Kenneth, et. al. *The Laborary Method of Changing and Learning: Theory and Applications.* Palo Alto, Calif.: Science & Behavior Books, 1975.

Bennis, Warren G. *Organization Development: Nature, Origins and Prospects.* Reading, Mass.: Addison-Wesley, 1969.

Bennis, Warren G., et. al. *The Planning of Change (3rd. Ed.)* New York: Holt, Rinehart & Winston, 1976.

Blake, Robert R., & Mouton, Jane Srygley. *Consultation.* Reading, Mass.: Addison-Wesley, 1976.

Blake, Robert R., and Mouton, Jane Srygley. *Diary of an OD Man.* Houston, Tx.: Gulf Publishing, 1976.

Blake, Robert R., & Mouton, Jane Srygley. *Building a Dynamic Corporation through Grid Organization Development.* Reading, Mass.: Addison-Wesley, 1969.

Bowers, David G., & Franklin, Jerome L. *Survey-Guided Development: Data Based Organization Change (Rev. Ed.).* La Jolla, Calif.: University Associates, 1977.

Bradford, Leland P. (Ed.). *Selected Readings Series One: Group Development.* Arlington, Va.: NTL Institute, 1961. (Out of Print.)

Bradford, Leland P. (Ed.). *Selected Readings Series Three: Human Forces in Teaching and Learning.* Arlington, Va.: NTL Institute, 1961. (Out of Print.)

Burke, W. Warner. *Contemporary Organizational Development.* Arlington, Va.: NTL Institute, 1972. (Out of Print.)

French, Wendell L., et al. *Organizational Development: Theory, Practice and Research.* Houston, Tx.: Business Publications, 1982.

Galbraith, Jay. *Designing Complex Organizations.* Reading, Mass.: Addison-Wesley, 1973.

Golembiewski, Robert. *Renewing Organizations.* Itasca, Ill.: Peacock, 1972.

Golembiewski, Robert, & Blumberg, Arthur. *Sensitivity Training and the Laboratory Approach.* Itasca, Ill.: Peacock, 1977.

Gray, Jerry, & Starke, Frederick. *Readings in Organizational Behavior: Concepts and Applications.* Columbus, Oh.: Merrill, 1976.

Hausser, Doris et al. *Survey-Guided Development: A Manual for Consultation (3 vols.).* La Jolla, Calif.: University Associates, 1977.

Hornstein, H.A., et al. *Social Interventions.* New York: Free Press, 1971.

Lawrence, Paul R., & Lorsch, Jay W. *Developing Organizations: Diagnosis and Action.* Reading, Mass.: Addison-Wesley, 1969.

Lippitt, Gordon (Ed.). *Selected Readings Series Two: Leadership in Action.* Arlington, Va.: NTL Institute, 1961. (Out of Print.)

Lippitt, Ronald, et al. *The Dynamics of Planned Change.* New York: Harcourt, Brace & World, 1958.

Lorsch, Jay W., & Barnes, Louis B. *Managers and Their Careers: Cases and Readings.* Homewood, Ill.: Richard D. Irwin, 1972.

Lorsch, Jay W., & Lawrence, Paul R. *Managing Group Intergroup Relations.* Homewood, Ill.: Richard D. Irwin, 1972.

Luthans, Fred, & Kreitner, Robert. *Organizational Behavior Modification.* Glenview, Ill.: Scott Foresman, 1975.

Mial, Dorthy, & Mial, H. Curtis (Eds.). *Selected Readings Series Four: Forces in Community Development.* Arlington, Va.: NTL Institute, 1961. (Out of Print.)

Pfeiffer, J. William, & Jones, John E. (Eds.). *Handbook of Structured Experiences for Human Relations Training (6 vols.).* La Jolla, Calif.: University Associates, 1977.

Pfeiffer, J. William, & Jones, John E. *Reference Guide to Handbooks and Annuals.* La Jolla, Calif.: University Associates, 1977.

Roeber, Richard J. *The Organization in a Changing Environment.* Reading, Mass.: Addison-Wesley, 1973.

Price, James L. *Organizational Effectiveness.* Homewood, Ill.: Richard D. Irwin, 1968.

Sargent, Alice G. *Beyond Sex Roles.* St. Paul, Minn.: West, 1977.

Steele, Fritz. *Physical Settings and Organizational Development.* Reading, Mass.: Addison-Wesley, 1973.

Walton, Richard E. *Confrontation and Third-Party Consultation.* Reading, Mass.: Addison-Wesley, 1969.

Watson, Goodwin. *Concepts for Social Change.* Arlington, Va.: NTL Institute, 1967. (Out of Print.)

Zaltman, Gerald, et al. (*Processes and Phenomena of Social Change.* New York: John Wiley & Sons, 1973.

Other NTL Publications

Reading Book For Human Relations Training

Edited by Lawrence Porter, Ed.D. and
Bernard Mohr, M.Ed.
$11.95 prepaid

This is the seventh edition of NTL's basic handbook of readings for laboratory participants and others who wish to understand laboratory experiences. Some of the articles were developed as theory sessions for various NTL workshops while others were written specifically for this book.

The Reading Book contains 33 articles, including the following:

- What Is Sensitivity Training?—by Charles Seashore
- Multicultural Perspectives in Human Relations Training— by Patricia Bidol and Richard Arima
- Using Feedback to Clear Up Misunderstandings in Important Relationships—by Barbara Benedict Bunker
- The Significance of Human Conflict—by Kenneth D. Benne
- Women in T Groups: Norms and Sex-Role Issues—by Rosabeth Moss Kanter
- Making the Choice to Live Full Time—by Bernard Mohr
- What To Observe in a Group—by Edgar H. Schein
- Confrontation and Basic Third-Party Functions—by Richard E. Walton
- The Learning's in the Flight, But the Payoff's in the Landing—by Larry Porter

The NTL Managers' Handbook

Edited by Roger A. Ritvo, Ph.D. and
Alice G. Sargent, Ed.D.
$17.00 prepaid

Written as a practical guide for managers, this new volume provides an important complement to NTL's successful professional and managerial development programs. The **Handbook** responds to the needs expressed by more than 6,000 "graduates" of these programs.

Organized into three sections, the **Handbook** focuses on laboratory education, the management of interpersonal relationships, and organizational and systems change. Its authors present strategies for planning and managing organization development and discuss the skills and values necessary for managerial effectiveness.

The **Handbook** contains 43 articles, including the following:

- Situational Leadership—by Kenneth H. Blanchard
- Managing the Computer Transition—by Saul Eisen and Ava Albert Schnidman
- Strategic Planning for Managers—by Peter B. Vaill
- Managing with Quality Circles—by Roger A. Ritvo
- Managing Diversity: What's In It for You?—by Nancy Brown
- Black Professionals and Organizational Stress—by David L. Ford, Jr.
- Building a Model of Managerial Effectiveness: A Competency-Based Approach—by Alice G. Sargent

Order from: **Publications Department**
NTL Institute
P.O. Box 9155, Rosslyn Station
Arlington, Virginia 22209